Creeksid

W9-BQY-511

Facing the Effects of Mother's Absence

HOME BY CHOICE

Brenda Hunter, Ph.D.

Facing the Effects of Mother's Absence

HOME BY CHOICE

Brenda Hunter, Ph.D.

MULTNOMAH

Portland, Oregon

Cover design by Durand Demlow

HOME BY CHOICE
©1991 by Brenda Hunter, Ph.D.
Published by Multnomah Press
10209 SE Division Street
Portland, Oregon 97266

Multnomah Press is a ministry of Multnomah School of the
Bible, 8435 NE Glisan Street, Portland, Oregon 97220.

Printed in the United States of America.

To contact the author or Home by Choice, write to:
Home by Choice, Inc.
P.O. Box 103
Vienna, VA 22183

Library of Congress Cataloging-in-Publication Data
Hunter, Brenda.
    Home by choice : facing the effects of mother's absence :
    creating emotional security in children / Brenda Hunter.
        p. cm.
    Includes index.
ISBN 0-88070-433-0
    1. Motherhood—United States. 2. Mothers—United
States—Psychology. 3. Mother and child—United States.
4. Security (Psychology) in children. I. Title.
HQ759.H848 1991
306.874'3—dc20   91-13625
                                                       CIP

91 92 93 94 95 96 97 98 99 - 10 9 8 7 6 5 4 3 2

Dedication

This book is dedicated to
every mother who is home by choice.
I applaud you for your courage—
your willingness to stay home at some personal cost—
and I support your conviction that you are
the best person to rear your child.
I have written this book for you.

Acknowledgments

I am a fortunate woman. Not only do I have a talented, multi-skilled family, but my husband and daughters have been my encouragers, my cheerleaders, through a long, arduous doctoral program, and, of late, through the writing of this book.

Additionally, Don and Holly edited the manuscript before my editor at Multnomah, Liz Heaney, ever saw it. Don worked with me on ideas and logic; Holly, on word choice and writing style. As the deadline approached, the three of us were up early and late, working as a team.

I also wish to thank Liz Heaney for her substantial contribution. After Liz saw the initial draft, she asked thoughtful, hard questions that sent me back to the library for a deeper, broader look. Because this book makes strong statements, it needed a strong, bright editor. I found that in Liz, and I am grateful.

Finally, I wish to thank the individuals who have allowed me to share their deeply personal stories. Some appear in the book under their own names; others simply gave me permission to share their pain, but anonymously. It was their hope—and mine—that by honestly sharing their struggles, they could help others find healing.

Contents

INTRODUCTION

The Inner Home

"Hello, is mother at home?"
No one is home today.
"But Father—he should be there."
No one—no one is here.
                    William Stafford

"In the ordinary course of events, a child
takes in love with his mother's milk."
                    Anthony Storr

Home. What diverse images and deep longings that
simple word conjures up. For some people, home is a war
zone where conflict reigns and the threat of violence
lingers in the air. For others home is a place of refuge and
repair, where solace is readily found and the restoration of
the self is possible. In homes such as these, both parents
love each other and allow their children to speak openly
about their feelings.

Yet for all too many, home is a stark, often empty abode
where a family occasionally gathers but where nurturance
is either grudgingly given or withheld. In this instance,

home becomes, as poet Robert Frost says in "The Death of the Hired Man," a place where "when you have to go there, they have to take you in."

As we grew up, we internalized a sense of home based on the way we were treated by our families. Sponge-like, we absorbed our home's emotional atmosphere through tone of voice, words of derision or encouragement, and the presence or absence of affection. While some of us were treated with love and respect, others of us were abused or neglected.

Robin remembers that as a teenager she slept with an overcoat thrown over the foot of her bed and her window ajar during the coldest Maine nights, ready to flee if she should hear the heavy, rapid footsteps of her father approaching her room. Many nights she went to bed trying to block out the sound of her parents' angry voices in the room beneath her, destroying each other's self-esteem. Too many nights Robin was awakened abruptly by a slap in the face. One of five children, only she served as the lightning rod for her father's unreasoning rage. Robin did not realize that her father, also abused as a child, was perpetuating a pattern of violent abuse. All she knew was that as a young adult she dreaded returning home, even at Christmas time, to again become the victim of his violence.

While even the thought of home generates anxiety for those of us who grew up in homes punctuated by violence, many of us viewed our childhood home as the best place to be. Home, for us, was a place where good things happened; it was a safe place of love, warmth, action, and laughter. Or as a Vietnam veteran has said: "At home I felt a sense of being protected. Nothing could happen to me there—no harm would come to me. Even if I was home alone, I still had that feeling."[1] Fortunate are those of us who had reasonably "whole" parents. Remembering a happy and secure childhood, we speak of our earliest home with great warmth and affection.

Phyllis, an opera singer with warm, compassionate eyes, grew up on an Iowa farm with her sister, Eleanor, and two parents who loved each other. Her father, a burly, soft-spoken farmer, and her mother, a red-haired librarian, loved and nurtured their daughters. Consequently, Phyllis internalized a rich, deep sense of "home" during her early years. "Even when my mother grew feeble in her eighties, long after my father had died and she had left the farm to move into town, I always felt I could go home if I needed to. I know this sounds crazy—after all, my mother was *old*—but she personified 'home' to me, and the thought that I could go home if life ever became unmanageable has always comforted me."

Having received sufficient love and nurture from both parents during her childhood, Phyllis has been "at home" on this earth throughout her fifty-four years. Moreover, she has been able to create a home for herself, her husband Larry, and for their two children. Says Larry, "Phyllis is the most secure person I have ever known."

Those of us, then, who have been well loved and nurtured by our parents possess a positive inner home. But what about those of us who were deprived of essential love and care, especially by our mothers, during our earliest months and years? According to British psychoanalyst Anthony Storr, while a loved child incorporates "a lively sense of his own value" that enables him to cope with life with a strong and happy heart, the child who is "unwanted, rejected or disapproved of" has no comparable inner strength. Says Storr, "although such a child may experience periods of both success and happiness, these will neither convince him that he is lovable nor finally prove to him that he is worthwhile."[2] He may feel a little homeless all his life.

Mary Beth, a forty-seven-year-old graphics designer, knows she missed something vital during her early years. "All my life, I've felt a deep emptiness inside. I guess when you aren't loved as a child, you grow up feeling that there is something wrong with you." Abandoned by her mother and father when she was a toddler, Mary Beth was raised by relatives. The middle-aged couple had already raised their own two children and were less than eager to begin all over again. "Oh, they fed me and gave me a place to live," says Mary Beth, "but they didn't give me what I so desperately needed—love and acceptance."

Parental rejection not only may generate adult depression, but the rejected child can grow up feeling alienated and alone. His heart's cry as he wanders from place to place is: "Is there any place on earth for me?"

Edward Lear, nineteenth-century British creator of nonsense verse, was abandoned to the care of his elder sister after the family split up because of the father's indebtedness.[3] Lear's mother never again involved herself in his upbringing even though the family was later reunited. Lear was "bewildered and hurt by her unaccountable rejection of him,"[4] and was subject to recurrent bouts of depression which he called "the Morbids." Having failed to establish intimate ties with his parents, Lear became a lonely adult, always searching for what he felt he had missed. He longed for "someone who would want him as a person in the way his parents had not wanted him as a child."[5]

Throughout his adult life Lear wandered from country to country, a nomadic existence typical of the maternally deprived. These souls find it "difficult to create a place which they consider 'home.'"[6]

"Children learn early in life," said the late British psychiatrist John Bowlby, addressing the American Psychiatric Association in 1986, "that life is either a gift to be enjoyed or a burden to be borne."

Is the child welcomed in the family by both parents and adequately nurtured? Does his mother sensitively respond to his signals in the early months and years of life, creating a sense of security? Or is the mother harried, preoccupied, or physically absent so that her baby comes to feel he cannot trust anyone to hear him or meet his needs?

Our children's sense of security—that's a lot to put at risk for any reason. Yet we are doing just this in America today by creating a cultural climate that wars against mother love.

For more than two decades mothering has been devalued in America. It has even become a status symbol for the modern woman to take as little time as possible away from work for full-time mothering. Some speak with pride of working up to the day of delivery and indicate they plan to be back in the office posthaste. One woman I met delivered her baby on Tuesday and was back at the office the following Friday.

Yet how can any mother create a sense of *home* for her baby in a few short weeks or months?

But there are other mothers—and their number is legion—who are home by choice providing their children with their continuous presence and love. These mothers are home because they know that they, and not a child care provider, can best nurture their children and give them a sense of home. They know that children thrive in their mother's presence and suffer from her prolonged, daily absences.

Some elect to stay home because they carry inside a rich, warm sense of home and wish to pass the good parenting on. Said one careerist who came home when her son was born, "I grew up in a large, close-knit family and I wish to pass the legacy on." Still others are home because they wish to give their children the sense of home they were denied. They grew up in dysfunctional families and refuse to perpetuate the generational cycle of inadequate nurture. Having worked through early neglect or rejection, these mothers strive to give their children a richer sense of home than they themselves experienced.

Writer Joyce Maynard is one of these. Writing in *Elle*, Maynard says that having experienced both an early dysfunctional family life and career success, she sought "a far more elusive and mysterious commodity—success on the home front and the security of home and family."[7]

It is possible to give our children more love and nurture than we received. It is also possible (as millions of families prove) for a mother to stay home to care for her family—even at great financial sacrifice.

With a voice that's beginning to be heard, men and women across this land are reaffirming the value of home and of their ultimate human connections. The home, recently viewed as a prison, is now being seen as a refuge for family members, beleaguered by the world, as well as a necessary school for life. Increasingly, child development experts are saying what many mothers and fathers have known all along—that to be fully human a child needs to be intensely loved and cared for by someone who won't "pack up and leave at five o'clock." That someone is the child's mother.

As we move across the threshold into the nineties, the ranks of mothers at home are swelling. Not only are countless women quietly at home nurturing their children, developing their gifts, forging their intimate connections, but others who have spent years in the work force are listening to the logic of the heart. They are coming home.

Is mother at home today?

Yes, increasingly, she is home.

------·❦·------

I have written this book to take a deeper look at mothering. Part 1 examines the psychological research on attachment, the emotional bond each baby forges with his parents—especially mother—early in life. Additionally, it looks at recent day care research, the genesis of the present cultural denigration of mothering, as well as provides a commentary on the needs of older children for mother's presence. Part 1 offers ammunition for the troops in the trenches, as well as evidence about the effects of mother's absence.

Part 2 is all about helping the mother at home get the most out of her life so that she can meet her children's needs. It addresses some of the problems she faces (isolation, depression, lack of husband's support), yet it also challenges a woman to develop her gifts and understand she is home only for a season. To illustrate we have "world enough and time" for nurturing children, I've written about women who've made significant contributions to their culture after age forty.

Finally, for consistency of style and ease of reading, the masculine has been used to include the feminine throughout this book.

PART ONE

Homeward Bound

Children are the anchors
that hold a mother to life.
Sophocles

Talk show host Sally Jessy Raphael was in her glory. Seated with her in the television studio, under the relentless glare of overhead spotlights, six mothers were heatedly engaged in debate—any TV host's dream. The controversial topic of the day? Working versus staying home. Three of the mothers had given up prestigious careers to come home while the other three had elected to combine career and motherhood.

As the women clamored for a chance to speak, one in her midthirties sat quietly. Sally Jessy addressed Helen Jackson directly: "You were slated to become the first female black astronaut, yet you gave it up. Why?"

"My oldest son was having trouble in school," said Helen. "He was severely withdrawn and depressed. He had failed sixth grade. My son was fast becoming a statistic. He was another black male headed for trouble." Helen told the television audience she had *willingly* relinquished her enviable career at NASA to become a full-time mother.

What made this woman feel that caring for her hurting child was more important than making history as the first black woman in space? Helen, who now has five children and lives with her second husband, John, in Boone's Hill, Tennessee, has a compelling story.

Her parents separated when she was young, and her mother was hospitalized for emotional illness when Helen was five. Helen's grandmother, who proved to be the most stable parental figure in her life, came to Alabama to care for Helen and her siblings. Throughout her childhood Helen lived in a variety of homes with different relatives. When she was fifteen, she moved in with her grandmother, a domestic, who left Helen alone while she worked during the week and came home only on weekends. Helen admits that during her adolescence she had to forage for food, sometimes stealing when she was hungry. Yet Helen's grandmother loved her and motivated her to achieve academically.

"My grandmother bought me a set of encyclopedias when I was eight," said Helen, "and she rewarded me with fifty cents for every 'A' I received on my report card. That was a lot of money for her to give." By the time Helen graduated from high school, she had won a scholarship to Massachusetts Institute of Technology. Instead of attending MIT, she married her first boyfriend and had three children in rapid succession. After her marriage ended, she enrolled as a full-time student at the University of the District of Columbia, and upon graduation she found a job with NASA. NASA later paid for her to attend Johns

Hopkins where she worked toward her graduate degree in electrical engineering.

During her years at NASA, Helen says she was an exhausted, employed mother who ran a disorganized household. Meanwhile, her oldest son Malik was floundering. "He was never a behavior problem," says Helen, "but he did sometimes sit in the closet during class. He would go for days without talking. I tried to solve his emotional problems by transferring him from school to school."

Unlike some parents who blame their child when he falters, Helen felt responsible for her son's failure. "After all, I went back to work when Malik was three weeks old. It really tore me up. I tried to find a babysitter close to work so that I could breastfeed him at lunch. But Malik had a lot of babysitters growing up. As a little boy he was never real bad, just timid and underweight."

Feeling compelled to come home, Helen told her second husband about her growing conviction that her children needed a full-time mother. John, then a graduate student, agreed with her and promptly got a job to support his family.

So Helen came home and began homeschooling her three older children. After only nine months of homeschooling, all three children had soared by two or more grade levels in all academic areas. Malik, who had previously performed at the fourth grade level, now tested at the ninth grade level. No longer withdrawn and depressed, he began to develop socially and in time became a leader among his friends at church. Passing his high school equivalency exam at age sixteen, Malik is currently a junior at the University of Alabama.

Under Helen's tutelage, all three finished high school

by age sixteen. Her daughter Baqiyyah, once an aggressive, difficult girl, has been the recipient of numerous honors and awards. Another son, Isa, attended a chemical engineering program in Oak Ridge, Tennessee. Interviewers for this program said he was the best adjusted student out of the forty-two attendees. And most recently, Isa won a scholarship to the University of Tennessee.

During the seven years that she has been at home, Helen has channeled her abundant energy into caring for her family. Not only has she educated her children, but she also helped her husband and children build their log house in Boone's Hill. Moreover, she and her husband have started an engineering firm in their home and Helen works on this joint venture in the evening.

A candid, open woman, Helen admits her family is far from perfect. She is grateful that her family, even with its problems, is far healthier than the one she grew up in. Has she any regrets that she traded a place on a space shuttle to come home for her children? "I'm not sorry that I gave up my career. Sure, I was doing my thing, but my kids were suffering. And I could never feel good if my children were unhappy."

The Swing Back Home

Helen is among the myriad women leaving the marketplace for home. The media calls this phenomenon "the swing back home." Some, like Helen, come home because a child is floundering; others are tired of being torn by the multiple demands of career and family.

Tanya Coble, thirty-six, spent ten years working as a secretary on Capitol Hill. Although she came home during the early months of her firstborn son's life, Tanya gradually returned to full-time employment. "After we bought our house, I was forced to go back to work full-time," says Tanya, who now has two small daughters as well. "I had to put Brandon in day care; he cried when I dropped him off and he didn't want to leave at the end of the day." Tanya says the day care worker used to bring Brandon to the window to wave goodbye to her as she pulled out of the driveway. Too often, her son turned his head, refusing to look at his mother.

"That really bothered me. I felt it was unnatural to leave my son every day. My husband Clyde and I knew that the hours we spent with Brandon each day weren't enough, so we both felt guilty. Also, I couldn't concentrate at work because I didn't really know how Brandon spent his day. Finally, I just couldn't stand it any longer, so I quit." Tanya admits her family has continued to struggle financially, but she has no regrets.

Another mother, Judy Dungan, thirty-eight, left her job as legislative director for an Illinois congressman when she learned she was pregnant with her second child. Judy's decision is not unusual. Numerous women who believe they can manage the demands of home, job, and a first child, no sweat, come to feel it is not worth it after the arrival of the second child. Judy admits: "I didn't think it was worth the time-pressure and fatigue."

Although she had reduced her work load to three days a week after her first daughter, Madeleine, was born, Judy made the decision to stay home full-time after Hillary's birth. Now she works from her home part-time as a fundraiser for the congressman.

Judy, who admits that several years ago she could not imagine being home full-time, says that now she can't imagine a return to work. Awaiting the birth of her third child in a few weeks, Judy watched Hillary hugging her doll and realized that Hillary is doing only what she has seen her mommy do. "That makes me feel I'm doing a good job," says Judy. "Besides, some things are beyond economics."

Secure Attachment: The Key to Emotional Health

Any woman who gives her child the love and nurture every child needs is giving him a priceless gift. She is shaping her child's self-concept and teaching him lessons about love and intimacy that last a lifetime.

In his 1969 book *Attachment*, British psychiatrist John Bowlby wrote about the centrality of the baby's emotional bond or attachment to his mother, which Bowlby believes is the "foundation stone of personality."[1] Bowlby states that "the young child's hunger for his mother's love and presence is as great as his hunger for food" and that her loss or absence "inevitably generates a powerful sense of loss and anger."[2]

Freud, writing years earlier, also emphasized the singular importance of the mother or mothering figure in the child's early life. In *Outline of Psychoanalysis*, he describes the relationship a young child has with his mother as "unique, without parallel, established unalterably for a whole lifetime as the first and strongest love object and as the prototype of all later love relationships for both sexes."[3]

This most powerful early relationship between a mother and her baby begins at the moment of birth. The formation of attachment—or the emotional bond between the mother and the baby—is a critical developmental issue during the first year of life.[4] Psychologists Alan Sroufe and Everett Waters call this enduring bond to mother a "psychological tether which binds infant and caregiver together."[5]

It is the baby's attachment to his mother that allows him to explore his environment with a feeling of safety, using the mother as a focal point of security or a "secure base."[6]

Not only does a child learn about love from his attachment to his mother, but he develops a sense of self-worth based on his attachment to both parents.[7] Simply put, if a child's parents are consistently loving and sensitive to his needs, the child incorporates the message: "I am loved, I am worthy, others will love me just as my parents love me." If, on the other hand, the child's parents are rejecting, emotionally inaccessible, or absent, then a child may come to feel: "I am unloved. Therefore, I am unworthy. How can I expect others to love me if my parents don't?"

Several years ago a television camera crew and interviewer came to my house to tape a program on infant day care. In the interview I spoke about the importance of secure parental attachment in the formation of a positive self-image. After the program had been taped, the young cameraman said, "You spoke about me today."

"How so?" I asked. (I have learned that nearly everyone personalizes the information on attachment.)

"I never felt either parent truly loved me, and I've always struggled with low self-esteem." Jim then recounted a bit of his family history. One of five sons of a New York City stockbroker, Jim attended prep school and failed miserably. Unable to win his mother's love (he never understood why she couldn't love him), he disappointed his ambitious and successful father by repeated academic failures. Jim then became a silent, depressed adolescent who left home in his late teens. Oppressed by suicidal thoughts, he traveled to Miami where he became involved with drugs and an Indian guru. Several years later Jim met and married René.

"How's your marriage?" I asked Jim at the end of his story.

"We're struggling," he said honestly. "It isn't easy for either of us to trust. We want to be close but we don't know how."

Jim's story illustrates a central premise of Bowlby's attachment theory: that the child who is unloved will have difficulty thinking well of himself and establishing intimacy with others later in life.

Parental Absence

But what about something that doesn't appear as toxic—parental absence? What happens when parents have the capacity to love their children but are absent due to death, divorce, or career demands? For a child, absence does not make the heart grow fonder. Instead, absence generates profound feelings of rejection and a yearning for love that can dominate the whole of life. Harvard psychiatrist Armand Nicholi says that those individuals who suffer from severe nonorganic emotional illness have one thing in common: all have experienced the "absence of a parent through death, divorce, a time demanding job or other reasons."[8] A parent's inaccessibility, either physically, emotionally, or both "can profoundly influence a child's emotional health."[9]

It matters that a mother is present, both physically and emotionally, during her child's early life. If she is lost in depression, or exhausted by the multiple demands of her life, or absent for long hours each day, her relationship with her child will be affected.

A Personal Statement

I know what it is to have a maternally deprived mother who is, even as I write, a wanderer upon the earth. My maternal grandmother, Martha Callie Bradford, died when my mother was four years old. One of eight children vying for the attention and affection of an alcoholic father, my mother, the second youngest child, missed out. In truth, there was little to be had. What care and affection mother did receive came not from the stepmother who eventually arrived to care for the brood, but from her older sister Geneva. Yet Geneva was only a few years older than my mother; she, herself a child, had little mothering to give. However, mother remained intensely bonded to her sister as long as Geneva lived. Married at eighteen, mother lost a second significant attachment when my father drowned some three years and two children later.

With her early legacy and this second tragic loss, my mother was unable to be a nurturing presence for me or my sister. In reality, the only sense of home and stability I received came from my paternal grandparents with whom I lived between the ages of two and five. Those three years were the heyday of my childhood. I roamed the farm with the security that came from knowing Granny was either in the house or garden and Granddaddy was driving the tractor or milking the cows. My granny said I often sang out, "Where's my granddaddy. Oh where can he be?" This man, my dearest childhood attachment, always had time for me. He was the one who stepped in to fill the void left by my deceased father and absent mother.

Even after I left the farm and went to live with my mother, I was never happier than when I boarded the bus for the farm. My granddaddy, a slight man with a jovial smile and a shock of wispy, white hair, clad in his perpetual overalls, would stand by the side of the road as the bus ground to a stop, waiting to take my hand and walk up the long, winding lane. When we entered the farm kitchen where

Granny stood, a tall woman clad in bonnet, faded cotton dress, and apron, concocting her mouthwatering pies and frying chicken, I knew I was *home*.

The farm, with its white frame house, red barn, and grove of sugar canes, remained a place of warm affection, open communication, and safety for me. I always had this extended family to return to on holidays. I spent every Christmas and a golden month each summer with these loved grandparents and my sister, Sandy. Sandy said recently that all her Christmas memories are happy ones because she and I were together, two siblings who are emotionally close to each other despite our life circumstances. (Sandy lived with our grandparents on the farm.)

With my own attachment history, it is not surprising that I struggled with feeling homeless most of my life or that I worked full-time when my daughters were infants. Research shows that our early parenting history influences marital choice, self-esteem, and our ability to be intimate with a spouse and children. It should not be surprising that a woman's earliest parental attachments also influence her willingness to separate from her baby.

Must History Repeat Itself?

Does this mean, however, that those of us who didn't receive the nurture we needed are trapped into repeating our own history? No—it is possible to give our children more than we received. The late psychoanalyst Selma Fraiberg noted it is not inevitable that parents pass on to their babies the suffering they experienced in childhood: "The parent says 'I want something better for my child than I have had' and he brings something better to his child. In this way we have all known young parents who have suffered poverty, brutality, death, desertion, and sometimes the full gamut of childhood horrors, who do not inflict their pain upon their children."[10] According to Fraiberg, what is central is that the parent remember the *feelings* from his own injured childhood, not just the *facts*. By remembering his feelings, the parent refrains from inflicting his past upon his child.[11]

This has, in great measure, been true for me.

As it happened, I was a mother long before I became a psychologist. Ironically, I, who refused to learn about child development in college, studied it as a woman in her forties when my children were nearly grown. Then older and wiser, I learned that babies are fascinating. They are born with some highly complex perceptual, emotional, and intellectual equipment, ready to learn about their world, ready to bond to their parents. I marvel at babies now—at how beautiful and smart they are—but I never considered staying home full-time with my own. I was, after all, the daughter of an employed mother and the daughter-in-law of a woman who earned a graduate degree in her fifties so that she could become a high school librarian. Though my mother-in-law had stayed home with her two sons when they were young, she never suggested I stay home with Holly and Kristen.

Like other intelligent, educated women, I felt I should be in the workplace. I didn't believe then that my continuous, daily presence was essential for my babies' emotional development. Had I been honest, I would have said that while I loved my children, I viewed them, not as life's invaluable gifts, but as small people I could wedge in around the edges of my life.

I did try staying home with Holly for several months, but I felt lonely, depressed, and empty. My husband

Thomas and I thought the best solution was to put Holly in child care so that I could find a job and function more adequately. So when Holly was nine months old, I went to work full-time teaching English at a local college.

Neither my husband nor I was aware that the birth of the first child is a significant psychological event in a woman's life. In giving birth, a woman suddenly confronts her parenting history. She reflects on *her* early childhood as she cares for her baby. Moreover, a woman identifies with her own mother when she becomes a mother for the first time.[12] This poses few problems if a woman has a warm, close, and loving tie with a mother who is emotionally healthy. Then a new mother will have a deep reservoir of maternal love to draw from, since she was herself well cared for. But what of the mother whose supply of mother love is nearly depleted or dry because of maternal deprivation? For this woman, mothering infants will not be easy. When the baby cries and demands constant attention during those early months, the new mother with a depleted reservoir may feel desperate.

In my case, I thought about my mother a lot. (She and I had never been emotionally close, but earlier I did not understand why.) I can still remember as a young girl watching a friend interact with her mother. Martha, who lived in the brick house next door, had a relationship with her mother that I simply could not fathom. These two people spoke an intimate language my mother and I had never learned. I envied Martha and spent as much time with her and her mother as they would allow. As I matured, I realized something was broken in my relationship with my mother, but I tried not to think too deeply about it.

Thus, when I became a mother for the first time, I

didn't have the emotional resources to manage full-time mothering. Also, Thomas, an intern on call every third night, often fell asleep right after dinner on those nights he was home. Without emotional support or significant inner resources, I willingly chose to go to work. How much better it was, I thought, to challenge students to read Shakespeare and love Chaucer than to stay home alone with Holly.

My self-esteem soared as I donned new clothes purchased in the preppie college shops in Chapel Hill. Now I had interesting conversations with coworkers and friends and was available for lunches out. Moreover, I could talk about my job when Thomas and I went to parties with other doctors and wives. Teaching gave my life structure, meaning, and exposure to stimulating people.

What about My Child?

How did Holly fare? Ah, there's the rub. She had three babysitters between the time she was nine and eighteen months old. I fired the first sitter because I worried about how many hours Holly spent alone in her crib while Mrs. Jones ironed my husband's uniforms and vigorously cleaned our apartment. I left the second sitter, an impassive older woman who lived next door, when I learned about a third woman who had been given the "babysitter stamp of approval" by a Duke University psychologist. As Thomas's internship neared its close, Holly went to Mrs. Tate's bungalow and became one of nine charges. (So much for staff-to-infant ratios.)

When my second daughter Kristen was born, my husband and I had moved to New Haven where he became a psychiatric resident at Yale. Since it was more difficult to cart two children to sitters and we had only one car, I stayed home most hours, teaching part-time at a community college some forty miles away. Having moved to a new locale with no emotional support, I felt myself tottering over the pit of depression. Within a year my marriage was in deep trouble: my husband wanted to marry someone else. Suddenly I was a single parent with two babies.

Ironically, at this time I began an inner journey that would eventually involve confrontation with my unnurtured past, my relationship with my mother, and the healing of my inner self—my sense of homelessness. Along the way, with each advance, I became a more sensitive, caring mother. During this time of turmoil, a simple event strengthened my resolve to come home to my children. One day when I stopped at Margaret McCarthy's to pick up the girls, Margaret walked me to the car, carrying twenty-month-old Kristen. As I reached for my daughter, she turned away from me and put her arms around Mrs. McCarthy's neck. I was stung. My child preferred the sitter to me. Years later I learned that often young children *do* establish attachment relationships with their babysitters and sometimes these ties are stronger than the parental bonds. From that moment, I determined I would do whatever I needed to do to become more emotionally accessible and win back my children's trust.

Within a year, I was on board an airplane in the middle of a summer night flying to London with my small, scared children, then two and four. Holly was confused and troubled at leaving our home and at having her father disappear. (He had taken a job in the Southwest.) I was frightened as well. I wasn't at all sure what I would find in London; all I knew was that I was pursuing a better lifestyle for myself and the children. I couldn't bear the lonely life in suburbia any longer.

Soon the three of us were nestled in a caring community, affiliated with L'Abri Fellowship, in Ealing, London, and I had what every mother at home needs daily: emotional support from other women. Two mothers of older children took the three of us under their wings. As Katie and Judy nurtured me, I was in turn able to nurture my daughters. No longer trapped alone in a suburban house, no longer living the frenetic life of the employed mother, I spent some time several days each week with those two new friends and with others in the L'Abri church community.

That was twenty years ago.

Out of my own unnurtured past I have come to care passionately about mothering and to believe that good mothering is "every child's birthright." But I am not naive. As a mother and a psychologist, I know that not every woman, whether she works or stays home, is emotionally equipped for the task of parenting. When my children were born, I was not capable of giving them the nurture they needed, so I ran from my deepest self. I went back to work.

Yet I believe in personality change and healing for the unnurtured self. Not only have I experienced this myself, but I have known other women who have confronted the wounded child within and gone on to achieve greater self-acceptance and wholeness. Not surprisingly, their relationships with their children and husbands became more intimate and less conflictual.

Let's examine in greater detail what the studies reveal about attachment and how the sensitive mother works her magic. How does she forge those intimate ties with her children—bonds that last a lifetime?

Forging Attachments

She shone for me like the Evening Star.
I loved her dearly—
but at a distance.
Sir Winston Churchill

The baby emerges from the darkness of her mother's womb into the brightly lit delivery room as her father watches—nervously, eagerly, proudly. "It's a girl," says the obstetrician, holding the baby aloft so the mother can see the result of nine months of pregnancy and seventeen hours of labor. "She's darling," the mother murmurs. "Just look at those chipmunk cheeks." The new mother glances at her husband, who smiles, nodding his affirmation. The baby starts to cry, and the doctor places her on her mother's abdomen to be caressed. "There, there, it's going to be okay," coos the mother to her daughter.

This woman and her baby are taking the first hesitant steps of what child psychiatrist Jack Raskin calls "a beautiful ballet." As the mother sensitively provides for her baby's physical needs, she and the baby will communicate with intricate interactions that involve sound, touch, imitation, facial expressions, and body language.

Like Raskin, child psychologist Evelyn Thoman believes that the apt metaphor for the dialogue that ensues between babies and their mothers is "the dance." According to Thoman, babies are "born dancing,"[1] which is the title of the book she has written with Sue Browder.

What does Thoman mean by this? The kind of dance she writes about "is a timeless form of communication, infinitely more complex, subtle, and meaningful than a polite ballroom waltz. The baby's dance—which is actually communication at its most basic—comprises rhythmic arm movements, eye shifts, head tilts, coos, cries, fusses, gazes, and dozens of other behaviors."[2] A baby moves rhythmically in response to his mother. Through her voice pitch, tempo, facial expressions, a mother communicates her emotional state to her baby and he dances synchronously in response to the messages he receives.

The late Boston University researcher William S. Condon found, in watching videotapes of mother-baby pairs, that babies danced rhythmically "in unison" with their mothers' words. Studying babies who were a few hours old, Dr. Condon and his colleague Dr. Louis Sander found that no matter what language the baby heard, a baby moved some part of his body in synchrony with human speech. For example, in the fraction of a second it took an adult to utter the "kk" sound of "come," one baby moved his head to the right, extended his elbow, rotated his right shoulder upward, his left shoulder outward, and circled the big toe of his left foot. Says Thoman, this is this baby's dance step for the sound "kk."[3]

A baby not only moves rhythmically to his mother's

speech and voice inflections, but newborns are also adept at imitation. At a psychology conference on infancy I attended several years ago, one researcher showed the audience photos of a baby, just a few days old, imitating the researcher's facial expressions. When the researcher made a big "O" with his mouth, the baby did the same. When the researcher stuck out his tongue, the baby followed suit.

Since a baby dances with his mother from birth, he needs a dependable and accessible partner—someone who picks up on the baby's signals and over time becomes skilled at decoding the messages the baby sends long before he is verbal.

Our Human Connections

As a mother and her baby engage in the "dance," the baby is establishing his first vital human connections. According to Bowlby, over the first year of life, but particularly between six and twelve months of age, every baby forges intimate bonds or attachment relationships with his mother first, then with his father.[4] Although Bowlby states that all babies (even abused babies) attach to both their parents, he believes in a hierarchy of relationships, with mother at the top of the pyramid. While the young child expands his world to include other attachments by the second year, the mother is the "touchstone," the one the baby goes to when he is tired, ill, or distressed.[5] Psychologist Michael Lamb found that until the second year, when a baby's upset he will usually make a beeline for his mother.[6]

While Bowlby advocates that the mother's role is primary, he acknowledges that fathers also play a vital role in child development.[7] Lamb, who has written extensively about the role of the father, agrees. Lamb says that in the early years fathers and mothers play different roles in a child's life: fathers become important attachment figures through playing with their children while mothers act as nurturers.[8]

Bowlby also notes that the child forms a different attachment relationship with each parent. A child may be securely attached to one parent and insecurely attached to the other.[9] One study found that children judged to be securely attached to both parents exhibited the most confidence and competence; those judged to be insecurely attached to both parents, the least.[10] Those children who had a secure relationship to one parent but not with the other fell midway between the other groups on their scores.

Both Parents Provide a Secure Base

Even though their roles differ, Bowlby believes that *both* parents provide their children with "a secure base from which a child or an adolescent can make sorties into the outside world and to which he can return, knowing that he will be welcomed, nourished physically and emotionally, comforted if distressed, reassured if frightened."[11] Bowlby adds it is only as children become confident that their parents are dependable that they can afford to explore their world and take essential risks.

I remember going to a local mall with my friend Jennifer and her two-year-old son, David. She and I sat in a small amphitheater while David sauntered off to explore his surroundings. David often looked back just to make sure his mother was still there. Finding that she was, he happily wandered up and down a few steps, observing the people passing by. But he never forgot about his mother for long. He didn't need to run back; he just wanted her in view. It was obvious that Jennifer was her son's secure base—the love of his life.

Bowlby writes that as children mature, they venture further from home and the secure base their parents provide, but they still check in from time to time. Even adolescents and young adults need parents to function as a secure base.[12]

This past summer our daughters Holly and Kristen, both in their early twenties, traveled to Europe together. Before they left, in the name of economy, Don and I decided they should call home only twice. After we received a few frantic letters about their near-emergencies, however, we relented, agreeing that funding frequent calls was a small price to pay for everyone's mental ease. Holly and Kristen still needed a secure base and were much more confident travelers knowing we could be reached fairly often by phone.

Both Parents Provide Patterns for Later Relationships

Not only do both parents function as the child's secure base (and the mother especially so at first), but *both* parents provide the child with a pattern, an emotional template, for all other intimate relationships. According to Bowlby, a young child forms "internal working models" of himself, his parental attachments, and his world out of the raw material of his parental relationships.[13] Based on the way his parents treat him, a child will form certain expectations about how others will treat him. If the parents are warm, loving, and emotionally accessible, the child comes to believe that *he* is lovable and worthy. As he matures, he will possess high self-esteem; he will be able to trust others and, later in life, have the capacity to be intimate with a spouse and children. Secure in his parental attachments, this individual will expect others to treat him the same way his parents have.

What about the child whose parents are rejecting, cold,

violent, or physically present but emotionally absent? Bowlby believes it is likely this child will come to view the world through the lens of mistrust. Having low self-esteem, such a child may suffer from profound feelings of unworthiness.[14] As he matures, the individual who is insecurely attached to his parents will probably have difficulty being close to those who matter most—a marriage partner and his own children.

What proof exists for the validity of Bowlby's internal working models? A number of researchers have found that the security or insecurity of a child's earliest attachment relationships relate to his later social competence and sense of personal worth. For example, children who are securely attached to their parents are more popular with peers as preschoolers and kindergartners than those found to be insecurely attached. Also, securely attached children have higher self-esteem and can cope better with life's problems.

What is more, securely attached children usually become cooperative preschoolers and kindergartners, able to forge friendships and adapt well in their school setting. Insecurely attached children often become either aggressive, hostile, and uncooperative with their peers or they retreat, becoming passive and withdrawn.

Ryan and Jonathon

I know two children who possess opposite characteristics, in part, because of their differing parental histories. Ryan, a five year old, saunters into his kindergarten class each morning with the *savoir faire* of a future statesman. "Hello, Johnny," he calls to another boy. "Good morning, Sally," he says to an approaching classmate. Ryan exudes self-confidence and good will.

Ryan's mother, Cecelia, who worked for a U.S. senator, left her job on Capitol Hill when Ryan was born. She says that other people often remark at his self-confidence. "They can't believe he's so at ease with adults and other children," she adds, laughing. Ryan's father, Chap, a statistician with the federal government, is convinced his son is destined for future leadership. "Why, he might even become president some day," he exclaims, amused at his own presumption.

While Ryan possesses the high self-esteem of the secure child, Jonathon is an angry, troubled little boy. During his first year of life, Jonathon's mother, Marlene, returned to work leaving Jonathon in a neighborhood day care center. Apparently, Jonathon tried to form attachments to the various child care providers, but no sooner had he forged a bond, than his caretaker left for a better job. After a while Jonathon didn't seem to care about forming ties at the center; rather he became the preschool bully, snatching toys from other children, hitting and kicking peers and teachers on occasion.

Jonathon's mother works as a CPA for a local accounting firm and his father is a young lawyer hoping to make partner in several years. Both feel guilty about mortgaging their son's early years, but they also feel trapped—they believe they need both incomes to fund their upper middle-class lifestyle. Marlene feels particularly uncomfortable each time she has to leave Jonathon and his father for her too frequent business trips.

Jonathon's parents have tried to ignore his hostility, but recently his kindergarten teacher called them in to say Jonathon has few friends and that he seldom cooperates with her or other adults. "You have an angry son," Mrs. Jacobs said quietly to Marlene and John. "I believe he needs more of your time and attention."

What's the prognosis for Ryan and Jonathon? Can their early experiences be easily erased, or is each likely to continue down a particular developmental pathway? While a number of attachment psychologists believe that change is possible, most agree that personality change is hard to achieve—that's why they are so concerned that parents get it right the first time around. Bowlby believes that once we form our mental expectations about how others will treat us, they exist outside our conscious awareness, resisting dramatic change.[15]

Even when we encounter others who treat us in more positive, loving ways than our parents, we have trouble believing this new treatment is either deserved or real. We revert to our old, familiar thoughts about ourselves and others and simply exclude new information, especially in the area of our key attachments. Bowlby says we practice "defensive exclusion"; that is, we reject information that doesn't fit our perceptions of ourselves.[16] Only the securely attached child updates incoming information.

For example, a child who is securely attached to his parents as a result of their consistent, affectionate care, will develop an unconscious belief that should he ever need help, a trustworthy individual will come to his aid. This strong conviction that the world is a friendly place occupied with helpful people gives the child confidence when he encounters stressful situations. He feels he can cope with what life sends.

Suppose, on the other hand, a child loses a parent to death or divorce? Or suppose one or both parents are rejecting? Or perhaps a parent tries to control the child's behavior by threatening abandonment? The child then develops quite different internal working models. He finds the world "comfortless" and people "unpredictable."

Bowlby believes this individual will eventually respond to life by "shrinking from it or by doing battle with it."[17]

Doug, an only child, grew up in an eastern middle-class family with two stable, responsible parents. He remembers feeling loved, always aware his parents were *there* when he needed them. Doug's father, a teacher, was as emotionally accessible as Doug's mom. "He was a good father; I knew he loved me," says Doug. "Both he and my mom encouraged me to talk about my feelings honestly. They were people I could trust." As an adult, Doug has confronted life with a trusting, confident demeanor. He expects others to treat him as his parents did—with kindness and respect—and he handles stress confidently and with resolve. In his marriage he is cooperative, and with his wife and children he is openhanded and affectionate.

Natasha, on the other hand, grew up with an alcoholic mother and a father who abandoned the family when Natasha was twelve. At thirty-five, Natasha often finds life overwhelming. Recently, her husband broke his leg, and Natasha had to care for him in addition to her two daughters. "Why does God do this to me?" she asks, feeling that an insensitive Providence has dealt her a series of nearly lethal blows. Never having received sufficient love and nurture as a child, Natasha feels unable to cope with the exigencies of life. In her mind, God—as well as others—bears the cold parental imprint.

Although some consider attachment theory the best-researched theory of child development,[18] and Bowlby as well as numerous other researchers believe our early parental attachments influence all others, attachment theory has its detractors. We will discuss this in greater detail in the next chapter.

Other Attachment Figures

At this juncture you might well ask, But what about other caregivers? Why isn't a grandmother or a father just as good as a *mother* when it comes to caring for a baby?

A child needs at least one person he trusts and feels is in charge. That figure is the baby's "touchstone"—the one he goes to when he is sick or frightened or sad. All others are secondary.[19] Bowlby has said that a child can establish a secure attachment relationship with any caregiver—as long as that person acts in a mothering way. In *A Secure Base* he has said fathers can be as effective as mothers if in the early months they act like mothers. What matters to the child is that he has a caretaker who is sensitive and consistent, one who loves him passionately. Only then will he feel loved and learn to love in return.[20]

But let's look for a moment at some of the implications of this. Suppose a child does spend most of his waking hours with a father, grandmother, or other relative he comes to love dearly. Who will become that child's psychological mother—the person he is closest to? When I asked one woman about her relationship with her mother, she replied, "Which mother?" Her mother had worked full-time when this woman was very young and she was closest to her grandmother who had cared for her. I wonder if most mothers are willing to play second (or even third) fiddle in their child's emotional life. Occasionally, children come to forge closer bonds with their babysitters than their parents. A recent study found that some children who spend long days in day care may be insecurely attached to mom and dad but securely attached to a young, sensitive caregiver.[21]

One woman, concerned about this very thing, deliberately

moved her daughter to a new caregiving situation every three or four months to prevent her from forming close ties to anyone save herself and her husband. The mother did this without any apparent concern that she might be playing havoc with her baby's emotional life.

Additionally, some mothers discover they are jealous of the closeness the father establishes with the child in families where role reversal has occurred. One mother who continued working after her son's birth said she envied her husband, a writer, who stood, holding their baby, waving goodbye as she climbed onto the bus. "It wasn't too many months," said Jan, "before I felt Tom knew more about Danny than I did."

Even if a woman is willing for her husband to assume the primary caregiving role, he is unlikely to remain at home over the long haul. An Australian study by Graeme Russell illustrates this.[22] Russell recruited fifty families in which both parents shared the caregiving responsibility. In some of these families the father stayed home while the mother worked. Although this arrangement seemed initially to work well, when Russell did a two year follow-up study of twenty-three of these families, he was disappointed with what he found. Only four of the families had maintained their nontraditional lifestyle. Why had these Mr. Moms gone back to work? Several said they were bored at home, some said they needed the money, and still others complained of lack of adult company, as well as pressure from their male peer group. What about the mothers in this study? They willingly reverted to their traditional roles because life at home was "less rushed and more relaxed." Moreover, they felt that the mother-child relationship was stronger after they returned home.

While it is advantageous for any child to have a more

involved father, complete role reversal is still rare and may not be long-lasting. As one psychologist said, "Men just aren't wired the same as women." In support of this, a southern university recently voted against parental leave for its male faculty members because the faculty committee felt the men would use their leave to stay home and publish. Working toward achieving tenure would prove more compelling than changing diapers. Furthermore, studies indicate that even when dads are more involved with their children than is normative, they are still *less* involved than the average mother.

So mother, it seems, is not off the hook.

No matter how much feminists have tried in the past two decades to erase sexual differences, biology dictates that a woman carry her baby inside her body until birth. Her breasts provide milk. (Her husband's never do.) Moreover, a woman's baby is programmed to fall in love with her. During that first year, a mother isn't just feeding, diapering, and playing with her baby. She is teaching him lessons about love and intimacy he needs to know his whole life long. If a mother is absent, he will fall in love, or try to, with whomever she has left in charge. A mother who elects to re-enter the work place needs to grapple with this and decide if she can live with the consequences.

The baby needs someone who will consistently meet his needs month after month. Psychologists generally agree that consistency of care is best in the earliest months. Who is less likely to pack up and quit the job of mothering than the child's mother?

Of course, if mother is depressed or preoccupied with her own painful past, her baby will not be able to dance with her and fall in love with her as he needs to. But does this mean, as is sometimes suggested, that a wounded mother should simply return to the marketplace since she finds full-time mothering so difficult? To suggest this simplistically implies that eight to ten hours in the workplace will "fix" whatever is wrong with mother psychologically and that she will be able to give her child sufficient love and care during the few hours she has left each day.

While it may be hard, and even painful, I believe it is far better for a mother to seek help through psychotherapy and work through her psychological problems while she devotes herself full-time to mothering. A new mother has a wonderful challenge: she has a reason (in the person of her baby) to confront her unnurtured past and grow as a person. Many women have done just this and their lives are richer for it.

Besides, too early other-than-mother care has its dark, problematic side. Since the early eighties researchers have found that about half of the babies who enter outside care in the first twelve months of life are insecurely attached to mother and/or father.

Let's examine this evidence on day care and attempt to understand why separation is hard for a baby.

Mother Care or Other Care?

My bias is that a woman's
most important role is being at home
to mother her small children.
T. Berry Brazelton

I met Betsy, a tall brunette in designer denim, at a friend's house on a cold December morning. As we stood drinking our coffee, I asked her if she planned to return to work.

"Oh, yes," said Betsy with enthusiasm, as she cradled her ten-day-old son in her arms. "I can't leave my job for long. My boss wouldn't like it. Anyway, I've only been with this firm for six months, so I can't take much time off. Besides, I've decided to put Eric in day care when he's three weeks old. I want him to be adequately socialized, so I'm planning to expose him to other children as soon as possible."

Betsy believed her baby needed to be socialized through contacts with other adults and children. What she did not know was that during his first year, her child needed a "close, continuous, and intimate" relationship with her far more than the company of others. Child development experts indicate that children do not engage in peer play until they are about two years old.

Babies need their mothers. They need them during their earliest years more than they need babysitters, toys, or the material comforts a second income will buy.

The Great Debate

Psychologists are divided on the issue of other-than-mother care. While many support full-time mothering in a child's earliest years of life, others seem more concerned about the employed mother's guilt. I once cornered a child-development expert to ask him about his outspoken support of the employed mother. I knew from reviewing his research that he had studied mother-infant interaction, so he knew about the importance of the "dance." Yet in media interviews he failed to say with any conviction that babies needed to be cared for by their mothers. When I told him about my concern for mothers at home and their need for support from the experts, he took two steps backward and replied, "Ah yes, but mothers who work feel *so* guilty."

Other psychologists are leery about becoming embroiled in political controversy such as maternal employment and infant day care. Recently I telephoned a researcher to ask him about the research he had conducted on infant day care. Although he was initially cordial, he instantly cooled when I told him the purpose of my call. Brusquely, he said he was *not* interested in being interviewed. "I've forgotten *everything* I ever knew about infancy," he snapped. (I later learned that he had been burned by the media, so he had reason to be wary of interviews.)

While some experts shun controversy, psychologist

Sandra Scarr, the .author of *Mother Care/Other Care*, has become an outspoken proponent of day care. One often reads some pithy comment in *The Wall Street Journal* or *The Washington Post* made by this well-known psychologist from the University of Virginia.

Dr. Scarr, herself an employed mother, believes children do not necessarily need to be cared for by their mothers at home. She writes that "day care can actually be good for children." She believes that "today's child," while sensitive to his environment, is nonetheless "resilient." Scarr suggests that bad experiences can readily be overcome by good experiences (contrary to Bowlby's notion of internal working models): "Today's child is not a china doll who breaks under the first environmental blow. Rather, our child is a tougher plastic doll; she resists breaking and recovers her shape, but she can be dented by later blows."[1]

Although Scarr is an advocate for children's resiliency, she does write about an unsettling experience involving her third child, Rebecca. Scarr, who employed babysitters because of her irregular hours and extensive travel as a university professor, returned home one day to find her eighteen month old crying. Her small daughter simply said, "Kathy hit me! Kathy hit me!" Scarr found large, red welts on her daughter's body. Says Scarr, "the sitter had beaten her badly."[2]

After she called the police and registered her complaint, Scarr learned this same babysitter had physically abused other small children whose parents had filed complaints, yet because no adult witnessed the abuse and could testify, the police told Scarr they were unable to prosecute. Scarr writes with obvious frustration, "No one was there to prevent the abuse or to testify about it."[3] The irony in her comment should not go unnoticed.

It is to prevent just this situation that many full-time mothers stay home with their very young children. They feel it is not always possible to effectively screen every sitter, and they don't want to pick up the pieces once abuse occurs.

The psychologist sounding the alarm today about maternal employment and infant day care is Jay Belsky, professor of human development at Penn State University. But this was not always the case. Belsky said in 1977 that he found little evidence of any negative effects of infant day care. When Belsky and his colleagues reviewed the research in both 1977 and in 1980, he concluded that "infant day care need not disrupt the child's emotional development."[4]

Belsky has since changed his mind. Based on research findings since 1980, Belsky has said that placing a baby in day care during his first year may erode his sense of trust and order in the world. This may also lead to later personality maladjustment. Belsky wrote in *Zero to Three*, "Children who initiated care in the first year, the evidence suggested to me, seemed at risk not only for insecurity but for heightened aggression, noncompliance, and possibly social withdrawal in the preschool and early school years."[5]

Also on this side of the debate, of course, is John Bowlby, who has even been accused of making employed mothers feel guilty. I once observed a young female physician holding a sleeping infant in her arms ask Bowlby when she could safely return to work. Bowlby, the only psychiatrist to have twice received the American Psychiatric Association's highest award, the Adolph Meyer award, did not equivocate in his answer: "I don't recommend at all that a mother return to work during the baby's first year. What's important," said Bowlby, "is what's optimal for the child, not what the mother can get away with."[6]

Bowlby acknowledged that young women who have promising careers face tough decisions when they have children, but he did not believe the answer for them was to attempt to do two jobs—manage both career and family. He did, in fact, understand the educated woman's dilemma. "The more brilliant the career, the greater the pressure," noted Bowlby. "Women in the professions are unlucky. The problem is more acute with them."

Pausing, Bowlby scanned the room filled with bright, young psychiatrists and remarked, "If you want a job done well, do it yourself."

Clearly, infant day care is a significant national concern. Infants currently represent the fastest growing segment of the day care population. Because of early day care, a significant number of the future generation will grow up without a close maternal bond and with an insecure attachment relationship with one or both parents. But before we examine some of the recent day care research in detail, let's review how the psychologists do this research in the first place.

The Strange Situation

In the late 1960s psychologist Mary Ainsworth, first a protégé and later a colleague of Bowlby's, created an ingenious laboratory experiment called the Strange Situation, currently the most important instrument used by psychologists to measure the attachment relationship an infant has with his parents. It is the instrument of choice in infant day care research.

Robert Karen says, "No one prior to Ainsworth had come upon a method of assessing relatedness. And no one before had found a way to assess how styles of parenting contributed to individual differences. Through this ingenious project, capping years of research, Ainsworth had begun her revolution."[7]

The Strange Situation consists of eight three minute episodes that provide a window into the attachment relationship a child has with his parents.[8]

Imagine, for a moment, that you are a psychologist sitting behind a one way mirror observing and coding maternal and child behavior. First, you will watch as a mother and baby are shown into a room (a university laboratory). The floor is covered with brightly colored, intriguing toys that engage the baby's immediate attention. In a few minutes a stranger (hired by the psychologist) enters and begins to chat with the mother. Most babies hardly notice, or if they do, are not alarmed. Soon, however, the mother abruptly leaves the room and the baby is alone with the stranger. While some babies appear not to notice and keep playing with the toys, others begin to whimper or cry openly. Fortunately, the mother returns within three minutes and the baby is mollified. But alas, the mother leaves again! And whereas the first time the baby was left with the stranger, this time he is left alone. He does not know his mother is waiting just behind the door.

What do babies do when mom leaves for the second time? Some show their independence and don't cry; others go berserk, crawling after the mother or running to the door. "*Mommeee, Mommeee,*" they shriek. Finally, mother returns. And it is this reunion, as well as the one before, that captures the attention of the psychologist.

How does the baby greet his mother? Does he ignore her and keep playing with his toys? Does he cry inconsolably no matter how much his mother tries to soothe him? Does he cease crying quickly and become interested in the toys around him once again?

What happens in the reunion episodes allows psychologists to evaluate the attachment relationship that a young child has with a parent. Based on the reunion episodes and other observed behavior, Ainsworth and her colleagues at Johns Hopkins identified three patterns of attachment: secure, anxious-resistant, and anxious-avoidant.[9]

Patterns of Attachment

Ainsworth found that the *securely attached child* crawls or moves toward his mother during the reunion episodes. This boy or girl wants to be picked up and comforted and protests if his mother tries to put him down too soon. Because he has found his mother trustworthy in the past, however, he is easily comforted and will eventually begin playing happily with the many toys in the laboratory. This child knows his mother can be counted on to meet his needs responsively and sensitively. According to Ainsworth, mothers of these babies have been "less rejecting, interfering and/or ignoring than the mothers of other infants."[10]

The *anxious-resistant child*, however, is angry at his mother for leaving him. Writes Robert Karen, "He is hooked by the fact that she does indeed come through on occasion. He picks up that she will respond sometimes—perhaps out of guilt—if he pleads and makes a big enough fuss. And so he is constantly trying to hold on to her or punish her for being unavailable. He is wildly addicted to her and to his efforts to make her change."[11] This baby has a mother who is inconsistently accessible and responsive.

During the Strange Situation, these babies are often inconsolable, finding it hard to stop crying once they become upset. Others are conspicuously passive. It is his mother's unpredictability that produces the child's anger. He must deal with behavior best described as "she loves me/she loves me not," and this makes him furious. I once asked Ainsworth which insecurely attached child concerned her most, and she replied the anxious-resistant baby.

What about the *anxious-avoidant child*? During the reunion episodes, this baby either ignores his mother or averts his gaze when she tries to catch his eye.[12] He does not want to be held and will squirm to get down if picked up. Usually he is not particularly distressed during the separation episodes, or if he is, he seems to be bothered that he is alone—not that his mother has left him.

What kind of mothering has the anxious-avoidant baby experienced? These babies have had rejecting mothers. These mothers have repulsed their babies' bids for comfort and attention; they simply did not enjoy physical contact with their babies.[13]

Robert Karen describes the avoidant child thus: "He becomes angry and distant (even though he remains no less attached). His pleas for attention have been painfully rejected and reaching out seems impossible. The child seems to say, Who needs you—I can do it on my own! Often in conjunction with this attitude grandiose ideas about the self develop: I am great, I don't need anybody."[14]

On the surface, the avoidant child personifies the American virtues of independence and individualism. He doesn't appear to need his mother at all. He is the kid who can be dropped off at the day care center and picked up *whenever*. And while the other children may look longingly toward the door, awaiting the vision of their mother's form, this child continues playing with toys. He is occupied, not with relationships, but with inanimate objects. He acts as if he has no needs. In actuality, the avoidant child has built a wall to protect a vulnerable self. For some, this wall will remain in place until someone comes along years later to dismantle it, stone by stone—possibly a psychiatrist or a trusted, patient spouse.

Mary Main, a psychologist who has pioneered attachment research on adults at the University of California at Berkeley, believes avoidance is a defense mechanism.[15] The avoidant child has been repulsed so many times by the one who should love and comfort him that he defends himself against further emotional pain by ignoring his mother in times of heightened stress and anxiety.

Think about this for a moment. Our babies come out of the womb frightfully dependent. We humans have the longest state of dependency of any of God's creatures; a baby needs *everything.* He needs to be fed, to have his diapers changed, and to be talked to if he's ever to learn language. All he can do, initially, to communicate is cry and flail about. If he's left to cry in his crib for long periods of time or if his mother is out of sync with him, he will be hurt and confused.

To protect himself, the baby withdraws. He avoids this mother he needs, but he is *angry.* That's a lot for a baby to have to process by twelve months of age.

The Pain that Is Separation

Let's look for a moment at an experience that conjures up powerful feelings in our babies—separation from parents, especially mothers. As Erik Larson wrote in *Parents* magazine: "Separation is serious business and psychologists now conduct their research with increasing urgency. They cite the large numbers of children who must cope with separation as their moms go back to work and as divorce breaks up more families."[16]

When Ricky's mother, Eva, initially left him in the neighborhood day care center, he sobbed as she walked out the door. Over the next four years, Ricky, who told his parents that he didn't like going to day care, ceased to show any emotion when his mother dropped him off and collected him at day's end. Throughout his childhood Ricky spent most of his waking hours at Wee People, and his sister, Janice, who had entered elementary school, spent her late afternoons there as well.

One day a clinical psychologist came to the center to get Janice to play with her daughter. As Janice put on her coat and said goodbye to Ricky, the psychologist noticed that though tears flowed down Ricky's cheeks, the little boy stood mutely by. He didn't even ask to accompany his sister on the outing.

This psychologist who works with troubled adolescents later told a colleague about this episode, saying that Ricky had already learned his efforts made little difference in his world. "Someday he may become a depressed teenager," she said, "and not know why. He will be suffering from 'learned helplessness,' having discovered early on that his crying, his attempts to bring his mother back, didn't work."

What Separation Feels Like

Why is separation so painful for small children? During his first year of life when the baby is forming an attachment to his mother (and father), he is also forming a mental image of her that will sustain him in her absence. This means the baby will happily accept substitute care until he begins to form an attachment to his mother (between six and twelve months of age). From then on, until he's two or three, no other substitute will do. Also at about eight months the baby begins to experience separation anxiety.[17]

When eight-month-old Joey's mother, Jacqueline, walks out the door, he does not yet have the capacity to know that she will return in two or ten hours; all he knows is that she is gone. Gone. This woman whom he loves passionately has simply disappeared from his life. Joey may also be frightened by this babysitter that his mother has left him with. Simultaneously, he has to cope with his mother's disappearance and stranger anxiety.

How do we know how babies think? Psychologist Jean Piaget studied babies' intellectual development and found that in the early months, babies will not actively search for toys and other objects when they disappear. If a six-month-old baby is looking at a toy and the toy is suddenly removed from sight, as far as the baby is concerned, the toy has disappeared forever. Out of sight, out of mind. Once the baby has developed a sense of object permanence, however, he will he make an active search for a missing toy or missing mother. Then if someone hides the toy, the child will look for it; if mom leaves the room, he will search for her. (Some psychologists feel that babies develop a sense of person permanence before they know that objects are permanent.[18])

Piaget also found that before the age of two, children do not form mental representations or symbols of missing objects. Think what this means for baby Joey. Until the end of his first year (and sometimes not before age two), a baby does not have a mental picture of his mother to comfort himself in her absence. Joey can't tell himself, "I love my mommy and mommy's coming back. Mommy has not left me for good." Joey's mom has simply disappeared.

Christopher Coe, a professor of psychology at the University of Wisconsin in Madison and pioneer in studies of how separation affects immune responses, offers this provocative statement about such separation: "We've radically altered the way we rear our children. It's just never happened in history that we've imposed such early separations of such a lasting duration. It's a big human experiment that may have a high price tag."[19]

Of course, all babies experience some separation. "But when separation imperils that early attachment," says Judith Viorst, "it is difficult to build confidence, to build trust, to acquire the conviction that throughout the course of our life we will—and deserve to—find others to meet our needs. And when our first connections are unreliable or broken or impaired, we may transfer that experience, and our responses to that experience, on to what we expect from our children, our friends, our marriage partner."[20] Viorst believes further that severe separations in early childhood can create "scars on the brain."

Psychologists do not know for sure if repeated, daily separations can be summed in a child's psyche to equal a severe separation. But the evidence is mounting that these separations do their damage—that the cost of separation in early childhood is high.

The Day Care Research

Just what does key infant day care research show? The evidence since 1980 indicates that when a baby is placed in substitute care, even good quality care such as nanny care, for twenty or more hours per week during his first year of life, he is at risk psychologically. If a mother returns to work during her baby's first year, there's a significant chance the child will be insecurely attached to mother and/or father.

Moreover, the results of this research show that the number of children who are insecurely attached to mother and/or father is rising. When Ainsworth and her colleagues were first doing attachment research in the sixties and seventies, only about a third of the children were insecurely attached. Now the figure has risen to about one-half in several important studies. With this in mind, let's look at several day care studies.

First, a 1983 study of the infants of middle-class families by Pamela Schwartz of the University of Michigan found that no matter what the child care arrangement, those who entered full-time child care before they were nine months old were more likely to avoid their mothers during the reunion episodes than those cared for by their mothers at home.[21]

This same increase in avoidance was found by researchers D. Wille and J. Jacobson in 1984 when they investigated forty-five eighteen-month-old children in Detroit. When these toddlers were studied using the Strange Situation, those who were classified as anxious-avoidant had spent about sixteen hours per week in child care; their securely attached counterparts had spent only five hours in care.[22] Psychiatrist Peter Barglow and his colleagues reported similar findings of increased avoidance in their study of affluent families in the Chicago area.[23]

Also, two studies have found that boys are particularly vulnerable when mother goes to work during that important first year. First, P. Lindsay Chase-Lansdale and Margaret Owen found in 1987 that when mothers returned to work when their babies were between two weeks and six months old, sons were more likely than daughters to be insecurely attached to their fathers.[24] Jay Belsky and Michael Rovine also found that boys who spend twenty or more hours per week in substitute care are more likely to be insecurely attached to both parents than those boys raised at home by their mothers.[25]

Why are boys insecurely attached to their *fathers* when mothers return to work? Chase-Lansdale and Owen suggest that when mothers work, fathers may respond to increased stress by being negative and harsh with their sons. These little boys may not receive the love and nurture from their fathers that they so obviously need.

Boys, it seems, may be especially vulnerable to feelings of emotional insecurity.

Long Term Effects of Infant Day Care

Studies such as the one conducted by J. C. Schwarz and his colleagues have shown that older children who entered day care before they were twelve months old are more physically and verbally abusive toward adults, less cooperative with grownups, and less tolerant of frustration than their counterparts who were cared for by their mothers.[26]

Another long term study of kindergartners and first graders found that those who had been in a high quality day care facility since they were three months old were more aggressive than those who had begun day care later on. These early care children were "more likely to . . . hit, kick, and push than children in the control group. Second, they were more likely to threaten, swear, and argue."[27] Teachers said that these early day care children did not have strategies for dealing with their angry feelings; instead of talking about how they felt or walking away, they lashed out.

One of the most provocative studies to date was conducted by psychologist Carolee Howes at UCLA.[28] In a study of eighty children, Howes looked at how they were affected over time by a number of factors: age of entry into day care, the quality of care received, and family characteristics. Howes found that children in low quality care as infants had the greatest difficulty with their peers when they became preschoolers. When they entered kindergarten, their teachers rated these children as more distractible, less task-oriented, and less considerate than later-entry children.

Possibly the most startling finding, however, had to do with what Jay Belsky has called "the power of influence."[29] Howes found that as toddlers, early care children were more influenced by their caregiver-teachers than were those cared for as infants by their mothers. This was not the case for those who entered day care after twelve months of age. Then the family was the most important socializing influence.

For a parent, this is sobering news, particularly to those who want to be the leading influence in their child's life. Moreover, as these insecure children grow up (and their numbers are rising), the ramifications for society are disturbing.

A number of psychologists are concerned about the massive human experiment currently underway. One psychologist has said that never before in American history have so many children been raised by strangers.

As we give our very young children to others to rear, what's at issue is not only their attachment to us, but also our power to influence them later on. That's a lot to put at risk for any reason.

Other Hazards of Day Care

Thus far in discussing day care I have focused on the child's emotional bond and the fact that too early day care puts the parental attachment relationships at risk. I have done so deliberately because this is the area of greatest concern for child development experts. If a child falters in his emotional development, he falters in life.

But what about other hazards? For one, day care is a breeding ground for disease—for children of any age. Children in day care are exposed to a host of diseases, ranging from bacterial meningitis to epiglottis, cyotmegalovirus, and hepatitis A. In addition, children in day care are at much higher risk for having gastrointestinal disease, especially diarrhea, than are home-reared children.[30] Add to that colds, ear infections, and other upper respiratory infections and the result is a child who's often sick.

Many children find the long day in day care oppressive, regimented, and antithetical to their needs as children.

Wendy Dreskin, who along with her husband, William, founded and directed a high quality day care center in San Francisco, became so concerned about the stressful effects of day care on the children that she and her husband closed their center. Dreskin felt the children missed their parents and had to deal with a day that was far "too long for them." The long day pushed some of the children, hungry for parental attention, over the edge. Dreskin says of one child: "One day when another little girl was sitting in a teacher's lap I heard Alison cry, 'I want teacher's lap.' When the other child did not move, Alison attacked her, raking her nails across the child's face. She reminded me of a starving urchin fighting for a scrap of bread."[31]

Dreskin explodes the myth that children stop crying the minute parents leave. She says this is often what directors tell the day care workers to say to make parents feel better.

Dreskin notes that at the end of the day the children

eagerly awaited the sound of mother's car coming up the hill. "The children would listen and say, 'Cathy, I hear your mother coming.' They were so anxious to be reunited with their mothers that they were tuned in to the motors in their parents' cars."[32]

In addition to the longing to be at home with their parents, one of the silent costs of years spent in highly regimented day care will be a longing for the freedom of lost childhood. Play is the work of childhood. To play freely children need unstructured time. They need to be able to concentrate on building houses with blocks, coloring, dressing their dolls, waging warfare without the constant interference and regimentation that day care requires. My daughter Kristen told me during the two years she attended day care half days she was bored and longed to come home directly after morning kindergarten. She was never happier than when I picked her up at 2:00 P.M. to take her home to play.

Guidelines for Other Care

Evidence suggests it is far better for very young children if mother stays home. But how long does a mother need to provide full-time care? Obviously, parents need guidelines as they think about child care.

At an infancy conference, I once asked the experts how long a mother should stay home with her infant. While one said, "as long as the mother wants to," the consensus was that a mother should stay home, if at all possible, until attachment was consolidated at two to three years of age.

Selma Fraiberg, famous for her intervention work with wounded mothers, would agree: "[A baby] can tolerate brief separations at two and a half more easily than he could at one year. But prolonged separations for several days will still create anxiety for him. This anxiety is a measure of his love and a measure of his incapacity, still at two and a half, to grasp fully the notion that mother, though not present, must be some place and will certainly return."[33]

Fraiberg believes that while a baby needs his mother most of the time before age three, "around age three, but sometimes later, most children can tolerate a half day's absence."[33] Once a child has learned to trust his mother, he can transfer some of that trust to others. As stated earlier, a child of three also has the cognitive capacity to know his absent mother will return. Moreover, at this stage of development, a child is interested in playing with other children.

But this may be small comfort to mothers employed ten to twelve hours per day. About this Fraiberg is clear: "When a child spends eleven or twelve hours of his waking day in the care of indifferent custodians, no parent and no educator can say the child's development is being promoted or enhanced, and common sense tells us that children are harmed by indifference."[35]

So, what's a mother to do—especially the single mother?

What About the Single Mother?

There are no easy answers for the single mother. Her lot is the hardest of all. I know. For five years I was a single mother, worried about all that my children were missing due to their father's absence; also, I was afraid my ex-husband would decide not to send the modest child-support check. Fortunately, the girls and I did receive child support regularly. Many single mothers are not so lucky. Too often a husband flees and leaves nothing behind except wounded children and a mountain of financial obligations.

It is almost a given that a single mother supplement her

support check or even support her family herself. But *is* it necessary that a single mother work full-time outside her home so that her children effectively lose both parents at the time of divorce? I don't believe so. It may be possible for a single mother to start a home-based business and be with her children either full-time or part-time.

One mother started a business cleaning houses when her husband left her with three sons ages seven, five, and one. She wanted to keep her baby with her and she felt she had few other marketable skills. Christine made this venture a success, displaying courage and ingenuity as she paid her bills and spent time with her children.

While it is not my intention to heap guilt on single mothers who find they must work, they need to be aware of how their children may be affected. You see, young children don't understand that the mother doesn't have a choice. I would challenge the single mother, if at all possible, to use her wits and ingenuity to turn her skills into profit at home (more about this later).

And Mothers in Traditional Families?

I believe a mother should try to stay home most of the time during the child's earliest years. If she is working and her child is disturbed by her absence, she needs to think about coming home. One woman who made this decision is Dana.

Dana was a sales representative for a Fortune 500 company and had a stable job to return to after Miriam was born. When her baby was just six weeks old and beginning to establish a routine, Dana went back to work. After all, her baby had already begun to sleep through the night, so Dana thought that Miriam could handle her daily absences just fine.

But when she began her long days at the sitter's house, Miriam cried most nights. "Miriam went ballistic after I went back to work, but I told myself that she was just a difficult baby. Truthfully, I didn't want to think about what was happening because my self-image was wrapped up in my job," says Dana.

She and her husband knew something was wrong when Miriam's temper tantrums gained intensity as she grew older. According to Dana, Miriam was capable of "biting, hitting, kicking, and spitting" for hours at a time. Also, Dana felt a growing awareness that she didn't really know her daughter.

When Miriam was three, the family moved from California to Virginia, and Dana decided not to go to work but to begin instead to get in touch with her daughter. Besides, both mother and daughter were exhausted by their fast-track lifestyle. "We slept for three months," says Dana, "and I spent the early days dealing with Miriam's behavior problems. I remember not getting out of my bathrobe one day as I spent hours teaching her not to slam the door."

It took Dana nine months to get close to her defiant little daughter. "Although she was still angry with me, she began responding and allowing me to be physically affectionate. I had tried to be affectionate earlier," says Dana, "but she pushed me away."

Are there residual problems from the early years in substitute care? Dana admits her daughter is still prone to tantrums and she also suffers from separation anxiety. Each morning when Dana drops her off at school, Miriam needs "twelve kisses and tons of hugs before she is ready to go."

Dana has been home now for four years and feels

comfortable with her relationship with her daughter. She is grateful that she came home when she did, and she is committed to being there for her child in the years ahead. Not only has she worked hard on repairing her relationship with her bright, sensitive child, but Dana has also had the courage to look at her own parenting history and seek healing.

One Family's Decision

Some of you may be struggling with this chapter and its message. You may be grappling with the attachment research for the first time, perhaps as you contemplate a return to work. Listen to one young mom describe her inner turmoil when she found herself in a similar place.

Lucille Brannock was ready to return to work when her son, Quest, was eight months old—until she attended a Home by Choice mothers' support group. I happened to be the speaker. As I explained some of the attachment findings to the mothers present, I noticed this produced distress in one of the women. I later learned that Lucille was angry during my presentation because I challenged her plans for her son's care. Lucille describes her intense feelings:

"I left the meeting in a muddle, yet from the intensity of my reaction I knew that deep inside something was wrong. While working was good for my self-esteem and good for us financially, it was not best for our son. My husband, Keith, and I did some serious talking and thinking. We came to see that while my career could be put on hold, there was no way mothering could be put on hold. Our child would grow up one way or another. But would he grow up secure in his mother's love and confident that she was *there* for him? Or would he grow up with the memory of a mother who left early each morning to return late at night? In the end we decided I would stay home.

"After we made this decision, I felt so relieved. It was as if a burden I hadn't known existed had rolled away. Moreover, I found I became a better mother. When I planned to return to work, it was as if I had to pack all my 'good mothering' into a finite time. Then if Quest had a bad day (as all babies do), I got uptight. After I decided to stay home, however, if we had a bad day I knew we could have plenty of other days—to play, cuddle, and relax together."

Lucille admits it hasn't been easy for her to stay home, particularly in metropolitan Washington, D.C., where the median income is around $50,000 and the majority of mothers work outside the home, but they haven't regretted their decision.

What about Quest? Lucille says he is a happy little boy, and she and Keith are proud of him. Now Quest has a new baby brother as a potential playmate. "We are satisfied with our lives," says Lucille. "What else is truly important?"

As we read Lucille's words, they may sound regressive or radical. After all, as one woman told me, "Women work today, not just for economic reasons. They feel devalued at home. The price they pay psychologically is just too high."

How did we get to the place in this country where the woman at home now occupies the place the working mother occupied in the fifties?

How did the housewife fall from grace?

Fall from Grace

> What I have seen in many full-time mothers
> gives me great pride in women. It has
> made me see that they come through the
> very difficult task of raising children riding
> only on a deep belief that what they are
> doing is worthy and important.
> *Deborah Fallows, Ph.D.*

During the past two decades, the American housewife has experienced a massive fall from grace. In their press for equality of the sexes, feminists in the sixties launched a wholesale assault on marriage and motherhood that continues today. The mother at home, once the keeper of the family dream, is now regarded by many as a pariah.

Listen to psychologist Michael Lamb articulate the current cultural attitude which he attributes to the women's liberation movement: "Just a generation ago, for example, the working mother (especially one with young children) was considered selfishly derelict in her maternal responsibility and her husband (if there was one) was considered a shamefully inadequate provider and/or a weak husband because he 'permitted' his wife to work."[1]

Now Lamb says women who want to maintain any feelings of self-worth feel they must be employed. He writes, "Especially in professional and middle class circles, it is often rather shameful to admit to being 'only a housewife and mother.'"[2] Housework and child care, Lamb adds, have been devalued. He warns that educated women may just become overprotective mothers if they stay home too long with growing children who need them less.

All of us—men and women alike—are influenced by others' opinions, especially by psychologists who have become the parenting experts. None of us is immune to the way others regard us. Psychologists note that all of us formulate a view of ourselves, even as very young children, based on the way others see us. This is what social psychologists call "the looking glass self."

If others value and respect us, then we will love and value ourselves. If others devalue us, or view us negatively, then it becomes much harder to maintain a consistently positive self-image.

Most Mothers Still Stay Home

Even though the mother at home feels devalued by her culture, is she, as the media contends, home alone?

Sara alternates between discouragement and anger when she reads in her women's magazines that some 62 percent of all mothers of children eighteen and under are working. "I'm twenty-five," she says softly, "and already I'm an anachronism." Sara has become even more discouraged since she learned demographers project that by the early nineties, some 86 percent of mothers will have entered the full-time labor force.

Statistics like these make Sara feel that if she continues

to stay home to care for her family, she will not only be woefully out of step with her culture, but she will also be part of a vanishing breed.

But are these statistics accurate? Two scholars at the American Enterprise Institute in Washington, D.C., think not. Douglas Besharov and Michelle Dally took a closer look at the U.S. Census Bureau and the Department of Labor (DOL) data.[3] They concluded that most mothers of children under eighteen still stay home.

How did the authors of this study arrive at this startling conclusion? In examining the 62 percent figure more closely, they found that only 41 percent of *all* mothers worked full-time throughout the year, 16 percent worked part-time, and 6 percent were unemployed and looking for work. When the researchers zeroed in on mothers of children under six, even fewer were in the market place. Of these, only 33 percent worked full-time and 15 percent part-time.

Yet even these figures were misleading. The term "full-time" does not mean, as one would expect, that a mother works fifty weeks each calendar year. Instead, DOL considers a mother a full-time worker if she is employed full-time for *any* period during the year. That means a mother who works forty hours per week at a local department store during the Christmas rush for gift money is classified as a *full-time working mother*. So not all "full-time working mothers" are the same—or even full-time, for that matter!

To better understand who's at work and who's on home base, let's look at the data breakdown. In this study, several different categories of employed mothers emerged. First, *those mothers living with their husbands*. Besharov and Dally note that nearly thirty-three million of *all* mothers of children eighteen and under are employed outside their homes. Of this number, just over twenty-five million (or 75 percent) are mothers living with their husbands. Of these moms, 39 percent work full-time and 18 percent part-time. *That means 61 percent of moms living with their husbands are either home full-time or part-time,* essentially living on a husband's income—what we call the traditional family. Contrary to what some contend, the traditional family is hardly a thing of the past.

When we look at *divorced mothers,* some 63 percent work full-time and 11 percent part-time. Even when their children are younger than six, half of all divorced mothers are employed full-time outside their homes. Only 14 percent are employed part-time (as opposed to 17 percent of married women).

Although a majority of divorced mothers are employed full-time, they constitute a small segment of the employed mother pool. Some 3.3 million divorced mothers with children under eighteen work outside their homes. That is, only 11 percent of the employed mother pool consists of divorced mothers.

It's important to note here that while the majority of divorced mothers do work fulltime, they are a small slice of the working mother pie. Yet policy makers concentrate on *their* need when constructing family policy. Should this occur?

This is not to say the divorced mother's needs should be ignored. Besharov and Dally report that the divorced mother has a hard lot. She is seldom granted alimony unless she is over fifty-five and the judge believes she is too old for employment. And slightly less than one-half of all divorced mothers are awarded child support in their separation agreements. That is why, say Besharov and Dally, a mother and her children experience a radical drop in their standard of living at the time of divorce while the divorced father maintains or improves his lifestyle. A California study, for example, found that a divorced father's standard of living increased 42 percent, while the former wife's and children's dropped 73 percent.

Never-married moms tend to stay home more often than their married or divorced counterparts. Only 29 percent worked full-time; 8 percent part-time. These moms worked substantially less than divorced mothers. Younger and less educated, they often become welfare recipients.

In sum, the authors of this study concluded that working mothers are not a homogeneous group and that family policy should reflect the very real differences in the amount of time American women work outside their homes.

The Intimidated Majority

Even though most mothers still stay home either full-time or part-time, many are not aware of this. The media has done its work all too well. Most women are startled when I tell them what Besharov and Dally's analysis reveals. Suddenly, these mothers at home realize they are not an endangered species. At the very worst, they are part of a silent majority—a misinformed, intimidated, silent majority.

Since the early sixties, feminists have largely controlled the public image of women. Mothers at home, who are impediments to the feminist agenda, have been largely ignored. In their thrust for subsidized child care, equal rights, and abortion rights, feminists have done violence to mothering with their constant proclamation that mothering is a "low status job." Barbara Ehrenreich, author of *The Worst Years of Our Lives*, says that feminism of the late 1980s can be classified as "women's rush to do the same foolish and benighted things that have traditionally occupied men."[4] Not only have modern women earned the right to function as men—with their nurturing capacities nullified—but housewifery has also been denigrated. Continues Ehrenreich, the things that have traditionally occupied women ("rearing children and keeping husbands in clean shirts") are only worth the minimum wage.

What's a Mother Worth?

This view of the value of services provided by the mother at home is erroneous. Sylvia Porter, a noted financial analyst, states that the twenty-five million full-time homemakers contribute billions to the economy each year, although their labor is not counted in the gross national product.[5]

While Porter notes the homemaker is "economically nonexistent," she adds that only the wealthiest families could pay for the services a mother provides for love: "Yet, without you the economy would be convulsed. You are more than cold statistics. Replacing the services you provide is out of reach except for the most affluent—and because the affluent already hire these services at premium pay, they are scarcely available in some communities."

Porter decided to calculate just how much the mother at home added to her family's economic well-being in four different cities. First, she assumed the typical mother at home works a minimum of twelve hours per day from the time her feet hit the floor in the morning until she puts her children to bed at night. Porter also assumed the mother at home performs a diverse list of tasks, from cooking and cleaning to sewing and chauffeuring.

After checking the costs of the homemaker's services in four cities—Greensboro, New York, Chicago, and Los

Angeles—Porter found the labor performed by a mother at home would cost a family $23,580 in Greensboro, $26,962 in Los Angeles, $27,538 in New York, and $28,735 in Chicago.

What services did Porter calculate a mother performs for her family? She calculated an hourly fee for nurse-maid, housekeeper, cook, dishwasher, laundress, food buyer, chauffeur, gardener, maintenance person, seam-stress, dietitian, and practical nurse. Porter said her hourly rates did "not begin to measure the full value of a housewife."

In a sense, even this analysis is demeaning to the mother at home because Porter only looked at relatively menial duties. She did not consider some of the higher status jobs *every* mother at home performs: coach, teacher, interior decorator, religious education instructor, and child psy-chologist, to name a few.

Sylvia Porter concludes her article saying no mother at home should allow anyone to belittle her role: "Your gov-ernment should give you a medal for productivity. Your family should appreciate and cherish you." Indeed. The mother at home is the unsung heroine in America today. Not only is she providing pricey, irreplaceable services for her family while she nurtures her children, but *she* is important to society at large.

I spoke with a politician recently who stated that society would greatly suffer without the charity that the mother at home provides—to the latch-key children in her neighbor-hood, to her church, to her children's school, to her polit-ical party. She keeps her eye on the home front and her finger on the nation's pulse.

Not only has the traditional mother's contribution to her family's needs and to society been largely ignored, but mothering is currently viewed as an extracurricular activity that anyone can do. This cuts away at the core of a mother's feeling that she is giving her children something valuable when she gives them her time and herself.

From Queen to Drone

Once the queen of the road as she drove her brood around in her 1950's station wagon, many mothers at home feel lonely, isolated, and devalued. Mothers at home complain of a lack of respect in a career-minded society. Debbie Mayer, a thirty-three-year-old mother, says she tells people she runs a home-based business. When she explains that rearing her two small children is her "business," she is treated with condescension. Her listeners smile and say, "Oh, you're a housewife."[6]

Even Bob Greene, contributing editor to *Esquire*, who praised his mother for willingly staying home with him and his siblings, doubts that she would make the same choice in our era. It's just too hard to stay home today, says Greene:

> Many women today, I think, would be afraid to live my mother's life. So much has happened, so much has changed, that for a smart and resourceful American woman to do what my mother did—to devote her life totally to her husband and children, and to fit in other things only when those things did not interfere with her home responsibilities—would seem not only confining, but a little dangerous, a little foolhardy. I think that even a woman who instinctively might want to lead my mother's life would feel pressured to reject it on principle.[7]

While Greene is very much a modern man living in a

post-feminist age, he can't stop praising his mother.
Lauding his mother as the smartest woman he knows,
Greene says she graduated from Wellesley College, Phi
Beta Kappa. He marvels that his mother defined herself as
a wife and mother. And, he notes, she was always home to
serve lunch for her three children. Although he can still
remember the safety and security he felt during those
lunches, Greene asks, "Why should an intelligent, ambitious woman be satisfied making egg salad sandwiches and
heating up cans of soup?"[8]

Greene is "grateful beyond words" for his mother's love
and presence during his happy childhood. However, he
can't imagine that a savvy woman today would make that
same choice.

Cultural Images and Images of the Self

I became aware of societal perceptions of mothers at
home when I started to write my second book, *Where Have
All the Mothers Gone?* After my daughters had left for school
in the morning and Don had driven to work, I went to the
library to do research for my book.

What I found in the late seventies was a wholesale deval-
uation of mothering. I read article after article that said
the modern housewife had experienced a painful loss of
self-esteem and felt she must defensively justify to a hostile
and unsympathetic world her decision to stay home. In the
eighties we witnessed an important shift in women's
responses to these cultural messages. Many left home.
Countless women said, "I will have it all. I can manage
home, job, and children. It is all a matter of time management, stress reduction, and guts." Hence, the evolution of
the myth of the superwoman.

An article in *Time* reflects current attitudes toward

mothering.[9] The magazine cover depicts a wood carving of a somber mother clutching her equally solemn baby with one hand and a briefcase with the other. This wood carving, by the artist Marisol, supposedly represents the mother/child duo of the nineties.

Writing the issue's lead article on women in the nineties, Claudia Wallis says, "the superwoman is weary, the young are complacent, but feminism is not dead. And, baby, there's still a long way to go." Wallis, like Friedan in her *Second Stage*, presses American women to forge ahead in their battle for equality—no matter what the price.

Wallis asks if women heading into the nineties, women who bought the feminist line in the sixties and seventies, concentrating on career and neglecting to have children, are burned out and nostalgic for the fifties: "Is the feminist movement—one of the great social revolutions of contemporary history—truly dead? Or is it merely stalled and in need of a little consciousness raising?"

Wallis notes many women blame the feminist movement for emphasizing the wrong issues—the Equal Rights Amendment, lesbian rights, hairy legs, bra burning. Moreover, many who bought the image of the superwoman discovered a careerist with a small child must make significant sacrifices. Wallis tells of one successful careerist, Carolyn LoGalbo-Goodfriend, the mother of a five-year-old and manager of over $300 million of Kraft accounts, who cornered Gloria Steinem at a party and asked, "Why didn't you tell us it was going to be like this?" To which Steinem responded, "Well, we didn't know."

Additionally, women nearing forty, who put their careers before family, are finding they are childless and demoralized because of it. Wallis quotes disenchanted

Elizabeth Mehren, forty-two, a writer for *The Los Angeles Times*, "Our generation was the human sacrifice. We believed the rhetoric. We could control our biological destiny. For a lot of us the clock ran out, and we discovered we couldn't control infertility."

In commenting on mothers at home, Wallis acknowledges that, like the Hindus, America has its own class of untouchables. Said one mother at home, "It's almost as if there's a caste system of employment, and motherhood is down there at the bottom." Wallis feeds this mentality with the sober message that women don't want to be housewives anymore. Mothering, says Wallis, is a "low status job." Hence, Wallis believes feminism has rendered a body blow to motherhood.

How should the mother at home respond to the media denigration of mothering? It might help to know that researchers have discovered that those women who value mothering more than careerism were themselves well-nurtured as children. And what about those women who prefer career? Studies show that many women who put career first felt they received little parental love and support as children, particularly from their fathers. Or if their fathers did give them emotional support, it was often at the expense of their relationships with their traditional mothers.

In looking at the whole issue of maternal employment in this country, I believe we have focused on the wrong issues. It is simpy not enough to look at all the pragmatic reasons for maternal employment, like economics, cultural pressures, and educational level. What about a mother's personal history?

A mother is, after all, an individual with an attachment

history. This means that her own early relationships with her parents will influence her decision to work or stay home with her children.

When we look at the psychological factors propelling women into the workforce, perhaps the working mother is not superwoman after all.

Why Do Women Reject Motherhood?

*If men could menstruate,
abortion would be a sacrament*
Gloria Steinem

As early as the 1970s, researchers were asking why some mothers chose to stay home while others opted for a career. What differences did they find between the two groups?

In 1971 Rhona and Robert Rapoport, a British husband and wife team, found that most of the employed mothers in their study grew up in families where they were "lonely, only children."[1] These homes were marked by tension and sometimes marital strife. Most did not have emotionally close relationships with both parents. Of the five women studied, two had conflictual relationships with their mothers, and a third with her father.

Another theme that emerged from seventies' research was the father's profound influence on his daughter's career decisions. Psychologist Laurel Oliver found that a warm, accepting relationship with her father encouraged the development of a daughter's femininity and the acceptance of the traditional life style.[2] That is, those daughters who felt emotionally close to their fathers identified with their stay-at-home mothers, and they wanted to stay home as well.

On the other hand, Margaret Hennig and Anne Jardin, in their famous study of twenty-five successful corporate climbers, found that women who excelled in business also reported close, supportive relationships with their fathers. In *The Managerial Woman* Hennig and Jardin wrote that the fathers in their study were nontraditional and counteracted traditional ideals of femininity in their daughters by encouraging them to achieve in the world of work. Most of the women in this study expressed the desire to outstrip their conventional mothers. Their fathers encouraged this mentality. The authors write that the fathers encouraged their daughters to experience life in ways their mothers had not.[3]

Not surprisingly, many of the women had negative views of their mothers: "They remember their mothers as comfortable necessities, 'warm, fluffy pillows,' who were not terribly exciting or magnetic."[4] One woman decided as an adolescent she didn't like women because they were "stupid." She spoke of adolescence as a time of "reducing dependency on my mother, by rejecting some of her—and other women's—traditional ideas about women's roles. My relationship with my Dad changed very little. Perhaps it broadened and deepened if anything. I was always a center of Dad's attention."[5] Another woman said of her traditional mother, "I wanted to be more of a person than my mother was."[6]

Why did these fathers disparage their wives as role models for their daughters? It is possible to speculate that these fathers had unsatisfying marriages and looked to their daughters for female companionship. The daughter may have, in a sense, supplanted her mother and, as a consequence, was encouraged by her father to emulate him rather than her mother. In their identification with their fathers, these successful women ended up rejecting their own mother's traditional lifestyle. As they climbed the corporate ladder, none married before the age of thirty-five. None ever bore children.

But is the rejection of a traditional lifestyle equated with the rejection of motherhood? Does identification with father and his careerism automatically mean that a woman rejects her feminine, nurturing self? Or is something else operative? Mary-Joan Gerson of the New School of Social Research investigated these issues.

In her study of 184 female undergraduates, those who wanted to become mothers reported that they had happy childhoods and especially warm relationships with both parents.[7] These college women had memories of mothers who enjoyed childrearing and devoted a lot of time and energy to their children's care. Their family life was also happy. Unlike the corporate achievers in Hennig and Jardin's study, we have no collusion here between father and daughter with the apparent rejection of mother. What about those women who wished to remain childless? Their earliest memories were of a lack of nurture from either parent.

Gerson also found that women in her study who espoused strongly feminist views had minimal desires to become mothers. "It may be that motherhood is associated with inferior status for liberated women."[8] But why? Did these feminists have unhappy traditional mothers who were dissatisfied with their roles? Gerson thinks this is a strong possibility. She concludes that women who are strongly motivated to remain childless for career achievement may be fleeing family life because of early impoverished lives.

Lack of Parental Nurture and Feminism

This view is supported by another psychologist's research. B. E. Lott studied undergraduate men and women, finding that those who wanted to become parents themselves experienced warm, nurturing parenting in early childhood.[9] Their fathers, as well as mothers, devoted a lot of time and energy to childrearing. When these men and women were asked their views on feminism, they were not in favor of women's liberation. The feminists in the study, on the other hand, were not interested in having children. Nor did they remember that either parent had been loving or involved during their childhood. Fathers received particularly low marks.

These studies indicate that an individual's own parenting history has a lot to do with his attitude toward parenting. Moreover, one's attitude toward parenting may affect his attitude toward feminism.

The implications of Hennig and Jardin's study is that women who identify with their fathers (and not their mothers) become avid careerists if their fathers reject the mother's traditional lifestyle. Also, as Gerson and Lott found, for a woman to wish to become a mother, she needs to have been well-nurtured as a child by both parents. If she was deprived of sufficient parental warmth and emotional support, she may wish to remain childless and feel, as some feminists, that marriage and the family are oppressive to women.

Attachment Histories of First-Time Mothers

Intrigued by these issues, in my own doctoral research I decided to investigate the relationship between a mother's memories of her earliest parental attachments and her decision to leave her firstborn baby to return to work. I wanted to look at a *mother's* attitudes about leaving her firstborn baby to return to work—her level of maternal separation anxiety as well as her attitudes toward career and motherhood. I chose to link the research in adult attachment with research in maternal employment—something that hadn't been done before.

So one summer I made my way into three metropolitan hospitals in the Washington, D.C., area, armed with a battery of questionnaires. My task was to convince some eighty-nine married careerists, many still in pain from their recent Caesarean deliveries, that they should participate in my study. Fortunately, most mothers I contacted agreed. So I had the wonderful experience of talking to all these women, some of whom had worked until the day of delivery, about first-time motherhood.

What did I learn from this project? First, let's look at those mothers who preferred to be employed rather than stay home. These twenty-three women had the highest scores of any group on father rejection. This is not to say their fathers actually rejected them, but rather they *remembered* them as rejecting. These moms also valued career more highly than did those moms who preferred to stay home, and they valued motherhood less.

What about those mothers who preferred to stay home with their babies? They reported positive, idealized memories of their mothers.

While it is possible only to speculate about what these findings mean, I believe women who prefer employment may be attempting to gain their fathers' love and approval by means of a career. These mothers indicated that, in childhood, they could not always trust or count on their fathers. According to Bowlby's attachment theory, those women who have had trouble trusting their fathers in childhood may have trouble trusting their husbands in adulthood. Remember—they learned "attitudes and expectancies" at their fathers' knees. Without trust, these new mothers would have difficulty depending on their husbands to provide for them financially after the birth of their first child—a time when most women feel dependent and vulnerable.

I also found the more a woman remembered feeling rejected by her father, the less she was interested in the mothering role. It is possible that early rejection by her father interferes with a woman's ability to focus on the highly feminine task of nurturing her child. For a woman to interrupt her career, she needs to feel comfortable with herself as a woman in relation to the men in her life: her father and her husband.

What about those who preferred to stay home and who idealized their mothers? While parent idealization may indicate personality maladjustment (the defensive blocking of painful memories), in my study I do not feel this was the case. I believe the home preference group consisted of conventional women who idealized mothering and thought positively about their own mothers. Several called their baby "a miracle" and "a blessing." Many mentioned closeness to their mothers and that their mothers had enjoyed staying home. A number came from large, Catholic families.

As stated earlier, the birth of the first child is a significant psychological event in a woman's life. Many of the women I interviewed were euphoric about motherhood. Several indicated they had never expected to feel such a strong desire to nurture their babies. One mother, overcome with emotion, started to cry when she looked at her baby. "I've always worked," she said, "but he's so helpless, so vulnerable. How could I possibly leave him?"

What if these women had never become mothers? Among those women who preferred employment, many said children were not essential for the fulfilled life. If they had children, fine. If not, they would have found other outlets for their nurturing needs—nieces, nephews, work. Said an attorney, "My life would have been complete [without children]. I am happily married. I have a good job. I would have missed motherhood, but it's hard to miss something you have never experienced."

This was not the case for the home preference mothers. Motherhood for them was an integral part of their life plan. Some had wanted to have children since they were very young. And many said they would have been devastated had they been childless.

These two groups of mothers also had significantly different attitudes toward separation from their first child. Even at two to five days postpartum, the mothers who preferred to stay home had greater anxiety about leaving their babies for work-related reasons than the employment preference mothers. Also, their belief that their babies needed *their exclusive care* increased over time. This was not true for those mothers who preferred to return to work. By the time their babies were four months old, these moms (all twenty-three had by this time returned to work) had significantly less anxiety about leaving their babies than did those mothers who preferred to stay home.

What's going on here? Why do these employed mothers have less separation anxiety? It may be that they deny their feelings so they can return to work with less guilt.

In speaking about mothers who withdraw from their babies emotionally—for work or military deployment—the well-known pediatrician T. Berry Brazelton said in *The Detroit Free Press* (January 27, 1991), "They withdraw not because they don't care, but because it hurts to care."

In sum, my study shows that a woman's memories of her earliest attachments are linked to her decision to leave her baby to return to the workplace. These findings indicate a woman does not work strictly for economic reasons or for self-fulfillment. She may wish to return to work because she's attempting to gain the paternal acceptance and approval she feels she has been denied. If, on the other hand, a woman had supportive parenting and a particularly positive relationship with her own mother in childhood, she may feel her child needs her and this comes before any career; in fact, she becomes increasingly anxious about leaving her child to return to work.

All of these studies suggest a woman's relationship with her parents may affect her desire to have children, her feelings about feminism, her investment in careerism and the mothering role, as well as her level of maternal separation anxiety. So when we read in the popular press that only superwomen can manage it all, we need to realize there are *chinks* in superwomen's armor. For a woman to view motherhood positively, she needs to have been well-nurtured as a child. Otherwise, she has no reservoir of parental love to draw from for the next generation.

Three Famous Feminists

It's one thing to read about psychological studies in the abstract; it's something else to see their meaning exemplified in real life. Let's look for a moment at some women who came from troubled families and who are ardent feminists, influencing current attitudes toward motherhood.

Betty, who felt like an outcast as an adolescent, grew up in a home where marital conflict reigned. She reached adulthood, furious at her rejecting mother.

Even as a child, Germaine felt sure that her mother never liked her.

Gloria, abandoned by her father, was left to care for her mother, a woman who was hospitalized for "anxiety neurosis."

So writes Marcia Cohen in *The Sisterhood.* In this book, Cohen looks not only at the flowering of the second wave of the feminist movement, but she examines the families of origin for three famous founders of modern feminism: Betty Friedan, Germaine Greer, and Gloria Steinem.

Betty Friedan, founder of the National Organization of Women, grew up in a household short on mother love. According to Betty's sister, Amy, their mother, Marion, had "a complete inability to nurture. . . . We really absolutely did not have a mother loving us."[10] Cohen remarks that Betty's mother was intensely critical of her and made Betty feel both unwanted and ugly. Said Betty's brother, "My mother still thinks Betty has worked as hard as she could to make herself as ugly as possible."[11] As an adult Betty went into psychoanalysis to work through her rage at her mother.

Not only did Betty Friedan have to contend with her mother's cutting remarks growing up, but she witnessed her parents' heated marital battles as well. Her father, Harry, had a difficult time funding the expensive upper middle-class lifestyle his wife Miriam demanded. "The children remember the arguments between their mother and father, remember Harry very angry, his face reddening, banging his fist on the table, storming out of the room."[12]

What was Friedan's response to her conflict-ridden family and her own lack of nurture? Although she did have children, she participated in a violent, abusive marriage. Also, she later wrote a book, articulating her own dissatisfaction with the housewife's lot, suggesting that all traditional women in America lived lives of "quiet desperation."

Friedan's marriage was punctuated by ugly verbal and physical battles. Shortly after Betty's children were born, "her marriage was growing stormy and during arguments, things, sugar bowls, books and the like—seemed to fly."[13] Friedan was later divorced, but not before she had published her now famous *The Feminine Mystique*. In this, Friedan said that educators, psychologists, and women's magazines—as well as Madison Avenue—conspired to keep women chained to home and hearth where they developed only half a self. She termed the isolated, suburban home "a comfortable concentration camp," with prisoners trapped inside. The rest, as they say, is history.

Betty Friedan was not the only important founder of the modern feminist movement to emerge from a dysfunctional, non-nurturing family. Australian born Germaine Greer, author of the rebellious *The Female Eunuch*, was born to an absent father and a mother who openly rejected her.

When Germaine was three, her father went off to war. It

was World War II and Reg Greer, an army intelligence offi-
cer, joined the Australian Air Force, returning years later,
visibly aged by the experience. Meanwhile, Germaine lived
with her mother, Peggy, who delighted in flirting with the
American servicemen who stopped off in Melbourne en
route to the Pacific. Germaine later wrote of women who
teased men sexually but failed to deliver promised favors.
Cohen writes: "Eventually Germaine Greer would analyze
flirtatious, manipulative behavior with her own dramatic
flourish. She would shock and entrance with her graceful,
philosophical account of warped female sexuality, labeling
it the performance of a 'female eunuch.' "[14] Was this perhaps a veiled attack on her mother?

According to Cohen, Germaine would come to describe
her childhood as filled with pain and humiliation. Not
only did her mother beat her viciously on occasion, but
she hit Germaine with "passion" and "for no good reason."
"If she lost a ball or coloring book, Peggy would never
allow her to have another. That was that. And so her imagi-
nation began to paint possibilities. Perhaps she was not
really her mother's child. She didn't feel like Peggy's child."[15]

In reflecting on her relationship with her mother,
Germaine said: "I thought about the children who did,
obviously, not only love their mothers, but actually like
them, hang out with them. . . . I thought they were faking,
I thought it was a thing you did for outsiders. You pretended
to be good chums."[16]

As Germaine grew older, the antagonism between mother
and daughter continued. Germaine, a bright woman who
later earned her doctorate at Cambridge University, was
forced by her mother to pay room and board as an adolescent. The summer Germaine was seventeen, however, she
was ill and not working.

Opening the refrigerator one day to pour herself a glass of milk, Germaine was stopped by her mother who said harshly, "Leave that alone. That's for my children."[17] Stung by her mother's overt rejection, Germaine immediately left the house taking only the clothes she had on. Forced to return home a month later, Germaine found her mother in the garden. Germaine has never forgotten her mother's first words upon her return: "Who let all the flies in? Oh, it's you. You're home."[18]

While Cohen's *The Sisterhood* chronicled Germaine Greer's maternal rejection, Greer herself reveals her paternal rejection in her latest book *Daddy, We Hardly Knew You.* Her father "never once" hugged her. "If I put my arms around him, he would grimace and pretend to shudder and put me from him. It was a joke, of course, a tiresome, hurtful, relentless, stupid joke. . . . I clung to the faith that he was not genuinely indifferent to me and did not really find me repulsive, although I never quite succeeded in banishing the fear of such a thing."[19]

Greer states that shortly before his death, her father accepted all the "kissing and hugging" from his nurses that he had never permitted her to give him. It is not surprising that Greer came to believe, "At bottom, I've always thought I was unlovable."[20]

Fellow feminist Gloria Steinem also experienced a lack of parental love and nurture. Her father was unable to keep a steady job, and he later abandoned his wife and daughter when Gloria was only eleven years old, several years after her mother had suffered from a nervous breakdown. From then on, Gloria not only coped with her father's absence, but also cared for her disturbed mother. The two lived in a run-down house overrun with rats. Writes Cohen: "The poverty was ugly and years later, after

Gloria had catapulted to stardom as one of New York's 'beautiful people,' she would talk about the rats, about waking up at night and pulling her toes in under the covers in fear, about actually being bitten by one of them."[21]

To deal with the pain and humiliation of living with a mentally ill mother who once painted the windows of the house black, Gloria developed a protective wall around herself, detaching herself from her impoverished existence and the embarrassment of her mother's condition.

As an adult Gloria wrote, "My ultimate protection was this: I was just passing through, a guest in the house."[22] Cohen notes that Steinem, like Greer, had fantasies that her biological parents were actually her foster parents and some day her real parents would arrive to rescue her from her painful existence.

John Bowlby states in *The Making and Breaking of Affectional Bonds* that when parents exact role reversal from their children—when they require their children to parent them—they create profound feelings of insecurity. The child becomes "a compulsive care giver" when the child has a mother "who due to depression or some other disability" is unable to care for the child while insisting the child care for her. Then the individual grows up believing "the only care he can ever receive is the care he gives himself."[23]

When parents act like children, and their children function as parents, the children come to deny their own needs for love and nurture. They may cry out, as did one young mother who experienced role reversal, "nobody took care of me," or they may become detached, as Steinem seems to have done, denying both their anger and their pain.

The point of this brief foray into the lives of these

influential feminists is to understand that all three came from troubled families. Friedan and Greer had openly rejecting mothers, and Steinem, an absent father and an emotionally ill mother.

While Friedan has been able to overcome her parenting history, to some extent, in mothering her own three children, Greer wrote in *The Female Eunuch* that she "despised women." That Gloria Steinem's father abandoned her and her sick mother helps us understand the origin of her pithy slogan, "A woman needs a man like a fish needs a bicycle."[24] It stands to reason that her mother's illness and her father's failure to love and care for her during her own vulnerable adolescence may have affected Steinem's views of marriage and parenting. While she has had lovers, Steinem has never had a husband.

Like Greer, Steinem has never had children though she has made her abortion famous.

How ironic that three unnurtured women with distorted views of men and marriage have influenced our current notions of family and motherhood. Speaking from their woundedness, these three have disparaged marriage and the traditional woman. Not only did they witness troubled marriages growing up, but Greer and Friedan had traditional mothers, but they were alienated from them. It's not hard to understand, then, why they would lash out at women who choose a traditional role.

Unfortunately, their ideas continue to influence family policy even as I write. Though Betty Friedan has attempted to soften her message in recent years, acknowledging that the feminist movement has largely ignored the importance of the family and women's maternal needs, countless mothers at home during the seventies and eighties struggled with low self-esteem in some measure because of feminism's disparagement of marriage and the traditional woman. And many continue to struggle today.

Obviously Betty Friedan touched a nerve when she published her *Feminine Mystique* in 1963. How else could she have sold 300,000 copies? That her book sounded the clarion call for thousands of disenchanted housewives cannot be denied.

And yet, as Dr. Deborah Fallows points out in her 1985 book *A Mother's Work*, part of the reason for this radical response was that at first blush the workplace seemed like a quick fix for all that ailed the woman at home. Writes Fallows: "On a personal level the work place seems to offer an answer for just about all the problems and complications of women's lives. . . . Dependent on your spouse? Get an income, become self-sufficient. No power to back up your opinion? Get equal power with a paycheck—money talks. Bored? Get out of the house and in with interesting people. . . . Lonely? Get out of the house and into an office."[25]

Only one thing was missing from feminist rhetoric, notes Fallows: the effect of a mother's absence upon her children.

That's a lot to ignore.

When I reflect on these three feminists's lives I feel compassion and anger. I feel compassion, particularly for Germaine Greer, who at fifty-one has taken an anguished look at her relationship with her father. Not only did Greer finally confront her father's rejection, but she discovered that his whole life was a lie: Reg Greer was not the man he had claimed to be. Greer found that her father had lied about his origins and had even taken a pseudonym. At the end of her search for her father's past (and love), Germaine felt devastated. She writes, "In finding him I lost him. Sleepless nights are long."[26]

Who would not feel sympathy for a woman who has looked at parental rejection with such rigor?

Yet I am angry that these women used their impressive intellects to shape social policy without first examining and understanding their own personal histories. A whole generation of women has marched to their misguided anti-marriage, anti-male, and anti-family music. Yet it is ultimately our own fault to have been so thoroughly influenced by feminist rhetoric without first looking at the origins of this rage.

In the end, we women have to look to our own families and ask what our children need. As we shall see, youth in this country have not flourished during the more than two decades of feminism.

Children, whether babies or teenagers, do not prosper when mother is absent.

Do Older Kids Need Mother at Home?

Today's children are living
a childhood of firsts.
Richard Louv

In 1989 the Roper Center polled some three thousand women on their attitudes toward maternity leave. Of those polled, 13 percent believed a mother needs to take six months off work when a child is born, 17 percent said she should stay home for the first year, 32 percent said a mother should be home with her child until he goes to school, and 7 percent believed mom should stay home until the child is grown.[1]

The results of this poll reveal that many women think mothers should be home with their children during the early years of life, but that older children can fend for themselves. The fact that seven million children, some as young as four years of age, return home daily to empty houses supports this idea.

While many mothers may feel that school age children can care for themselves, their children do not agree. As *Time* says "America's children are struggling for sanity."[2] *Time* chronicles the slide of many of our nation's children into deepening despair. Suicides among fifteen- to nineteen-year-olds have tripled since 1960, and hospitalizations for mental disorders have risen dramatically (from 81,500 to 112,00 between 1980 and 1986). Even 30 percent of infants eighteen months and younger are showing signs of mental anguish, from withdrawal to anxiety attacks.

A recent Ann Landers column echoed this refrain.[3] According to Ann Landers the homicide rate has doubled among ten- to fourteen-year-olds during the past twenty years and most ten- to nineteen-year-old homicide victims are killed with guns. In 1987 alone two-thirds of all adolescent murders involved firearms. Child abuse and neglect have also risen dramatically—74 percent in the past ten years.

Ann Landers also states that two out of three boys and one-half the girls are sexually active by the time they reach eighteen. And one out of four of these sexually active adolescents will contract a sexually transmitted disease by the time graduation rolls around.

Ann Landers's column ends with a warning: "Parents need to wake up and pay more attention to their children." And *Time* concludes its commentary on the mental anguish of the young with this comment: "Parents must spend more time with sons and daughters and give them the attention and love they need."[4]

What's the Bottom Line?

Our children need continuing parental care to have a sense of wholeness. They need someone at home who's passionately concerned about them, not just during the early years but over the long haul. Even beyond infancy and toddlerhood, children need *someone* to be present during most of the hours they are at home. *Someone* needs to be available on a daily basis to educate, love, nurture, discipline, and guide. It is my conviction that that someone is mom. If a mother wants to rear a child who will leave home with a sturdy sense of self, she needs to be there for her child during his growing up years. Mothering is simply not a job she can turn over to babysitters or teachers or to the child himself.

In *Childhood's Future*, journalist Richard Louv writes about modern families. A columnist for the *San Diego Union*, Louv interviewed some three thousand parents, children, teachers, and other professionals across American. His findings are sobering: America's children feel a pervasive sense of sadness, due to a fragmented family life. Many of the children interviewed lamented the absence of family meals, family rituals, the loneliness of coming home to an empty house. Many children felt abandoned by their harried, super-busy parents. A common refrain among the parents was, "I'll play with you tomorrow."[5]

Said one third-grade girl, "My parents say, 'I'll spend time with you tomorrow,' but they don't."

Said a boy, "My dad works morning till night, and my mom often works afternoons and nights, so they say, 'Tomorrow we're gonna do something,' but tomorrow comes and they go to work."[6]

The children in Louv's book spoke poignantly of parents who left just as the children returned home from school, of turning to gangs or early sexual partners for companionship and solace.

One child was mature enough to recognize that his younger sibling was out of control because their mother worked during her second son's early years and their father was often absent. Said this boy, "My brother's morals and mine are different because my parents brought me up and my brother is getting brought up by a lot of his friends, along with me."[7]

According to Louv, increasing numbers of American children are raising themselves. He calls those who come home daily to empty houses, "children who own themselves." Although he notes that older children generally are positive about self-care, parents are embarrassed when they pick up their kids at the school or library late in the day. Many feel the judgment of the librarian or school teacher. One librarian spoke of her unease at locking the library doors at night while youngsters waited in the dark for working parents to pick them up.

The Latchkey Child

But not all children like coming home to empty houses. I didn't. From the age of seven onwards I came home to an empty apartment after school. In her defense, my mother was a widow who had to work. Since we had no car, she often walked the two miles home on her split-shift days as a telephone operator to be with me when I got home. I was grateful on those occasions when mother was home after school. Unfortunately, she would often have to walk back to work while I kept my lonely and frightening vigil at home alone, sometimes until ten o'clock at night.

Most days, however, my mother was at the telephone office as I let myself into our three-room duplex. The living room was invariably in shadows, no matter how sunny the weather outside—and I was afraid. I searched under the bed, in the closet, and behind doors before I relaxed. Since this was the late forties, I had no phone friend to call to share my news and worries.

"Hello, Phone Friend."

"My teacher said to call if I hear a strange noise."

"What did you hear?"

"The door knocked and I thought somebody was in there."

"Are you on your own right now?"

"Yeah."

"Do you want me to hold on while you check the doors and windows?"

"Yeah."

A couple of minutes pass.

"I'm back. There's nobody there."

"I think you were very sensible to call."

"Okay. Bye."[8]

Sometimes I called my mother at work, but most days I told no one about that day's events. I became a girl who seldom revealed her private thoughts or feelings. I did not share my feelings with friends or with my preoccupied mother. Sometimes I spoke honestly to my sister when I visited my grandparents where Sandy lived, but most of the time I hid my vulnerable self behind silence or superficial friendliness.

I did glean one important legacy from those years. When my own children entered school (after my values had changed at L'Abri and I became more emotionally involved in mothering), I determined they would not become latchkey children. I would be present most of the time so they would have a mother to talk to. I believed any child, whether seven or seventeen, needed to have a mother to listen to words spoken from the heart. Once our children enter school, they become citizens of a rough, tough world, and few can manage all the assaults on self-esteem alone.

School: A War Zone

Jenny, a tall, thin girl with thick glasses, walks to her junior high school blocks away from her home in a New Jersey lakeside community. She becomes aware she is being followed by two girls. Slowing down, she decides to wait and walk with them when they chant in unison, "Jenny, Jenny, who cut your hair? Bet you got it cut by a lawn mower." Jenny is stung. She walks quickly, hoping she can disappear inside the school before she starts to cry.

Henry, eleven, has a facial scar from an automobile accident when he was five. One day as he walks into his fifth-grade classroom, another boy hails him, "Hey, Scarface. Where'd you get that ugly scar?" Henry drops in his seat and tries to become invisible.

Roland, fourteen, boards a school bus on a fall afternoon in rural Ohio. His unruly hair sticks up from the crown of his head. "Alfalfa, Alfalfa," teases one of the popular girls. Roland's heart beats fast and he pretends not to notice. Others smell the scent of wounded prey and begin chanting, "Alfalfa, Alfalfa, what's wrong with your hair?"

Nancy, twelve, sits down at her table in the lunchroom with her four friends, only to be told by the ring leader that she can't sit with them anymore. The other girls giggle. Nancy feels a stab of fear. Where can she go? All the other tables are occupied by cliques. She sits down with the girls who have just rejected her and silently, painfully eats her lunch.

My husband, Don, recently took me to the small town of Clinton, Illinois, to show me the grain silo beside the rail-road track where two twins, Merle and Berle, waited to beat him up. They only did this once because Don later outwitted them, but he clearly remembers the fear he tasted.

These are real tales from the war zone called school. It's the nature of the beast for some children to torment oth-ers. Once our children enter school, they often need us at home to shore up wounded self-esteem. Psychologist David Elkind told a radio audience that once he had trimmed the edges of his picture in what he thought was an artistic manner until his teacher said, "Why did you ruin it?" Elkind, a professor of child development at Tufts University, said, "I never took up art again."

If we aren't there when our school-age children return home, we may never hear about the pressures or triumphs of the day. Many mothers find that by the time they arrive home at five or six o'clock from work, aerobics, or volun-teer activities, their children's hearts are closed to them.

Don used to ask the girls to wait until dinnertime so he didn't have to hear warmed-over news. He felt, and rightly so, that Holly and Kristen were reluctant to recount the news of their day twice, having told me earlier. I explained that Holly and Kristen couldn't sit on hurt feelings or exu-berance for hours after coming home. But that's what hap-pens when a mother is absent. The child then learns to internalize his feelings. Said one executive, "I was always alone in the house. I never felt my parents were interested in me. They both worked long hours. Now it's hard for me to tell anyone what's going on inside."

I believe one of the most valuable gifts any mother can give her child is the sense that she cares passionately about him and that the child's concerns are her concerns. If a mother does this, she will become not only emotionally close to her child, creating a foundation for closeness when the child grows up, but she will protect her child against susceptibility to later drug abuse and self-destructive behavior.

Drug Use and Emotionally Distant Parents

Armand Nicholi, who has conducted research on drug users, says that young people who use drugs have one thing in common: emotional distance from their parents.[9] Also, drug users spend a lot of time away from home, relying on peers for emotional support. Other studies of drug users, says Nicholi, show they differ markedly from nonusers; drug users come from homes where parents smoke, drink, or use psychoactive drugs.

Nicholi believes that when children use drugs (and some begin to use marijuana in sixth grade), it's because they feel lonely or isolated and suffer from "a moral and spiritual void. In essence, people take these drugs to alter or escape from a less than tolerable reality," says Nicholi, "and to meet intense emotional needs."[10] Where do these "intense emotional needs" originate? Nicholi blames parental absence, due to divorce, death, or a time-demanding job. Parental absence contributes to "the anger, the rebelliousness, low self-esteem, depression and anti-social behavior" of the drug user.[11]

Another study noted that eighth graders who were home alone for eleven or more hours per week were *twice* as likely to engage in heavy use of alcohol, tobacco, and marijuana than those teens who had a parent home after school. This pattern persisted even when the sex, social status, and ethnicity of the child were considered. Why were these latchkey children more susceptible to substance abuse? With nobody home, teens turned to their peers who led them astray.[12] So even adolescents need a sensitive parent to supervise and listen after school.

But a mother is not only a sensitive, empathic presence in her child's life. She is also her child's first teacher and, along with the child's father, the transmitter of cultural values and discipline.

Mother as First Teacher

I determined when Holly and Kristen were young to expose them to excellent children's literature. I knew the best way to foster reading and writing skills was to read aloud to the children as well as to provide an intellectually stimulating environment. I was better able to do this, of course, when I stopped working full-time and could better concentrate on the children's needs.

When each girl was one, I sat beside her on the couch and opened the beautifully illustrated Mother Goose. We began her education with nursery rhymes. Sometimes I made up tunes and sang favorite rhymes. I read as long as the girls would sit still. Eventually this evolved into the ritual of reading for a half hour before bedtime. Over the years we worked our way through anthologies of Bible stories, poetry, C.S. Lewis's Narnia tales, and classics such as *Heidi*, *Little Women*, and *Wind in the Willows*, to name a few. I loved those warm, happy moments. It was wonderful to have the girls lean into me and feel their warm, cuddly bodies as we read stories that no one had ever read to me when I was a child. What a marvelous opportunity to fill in some of the holes in my education, and what a nurturing experience it proved for all of us!

After Don and I married, he joined us for the nightly reading, taking turns reading aloud. We sat through years of evenings, four upon the couch, sitting close together as Don read *Two Years Before the Mast, The Swiss Family Robinson, A Christmas Carol, Pilgrim's Progress,* and *Robinson Crusoe,* among others. When he read *Uncle Tom's Cabin,* the girls and I wept over Tom's death. This ritual of reading aloud continued year upon year until the girls reached junior high.

What did this practice do for the girls? By the time Holly and Kristen entered school, each had a jump-start academically. Reading to children is a fine way to increase their vocabulary, encourage their imaginations, and expose them to great literature. And once a child has an academic advantage, he is likely to maintain it over the years.

I am not suggesting all children will become scholars if they grow up in families that value books and reading. Often our children have different gifts, just as we do. But whether our children possess mechanical, musical, mathematical, athletic, or artistic skills, all can profit from a time of structured family reading. The person who is exposed to great literature early on will grow up with a larger world view, an appreciation for the arts, and an understanding of human nature he otherwise might not have. Also, he is likely to read to his own children when he becomes a parent.

In addition to reading aloud, when the girls were four and six, I bought each a weekly paperback. I was influenced in this decision by a friend who is now a university professor in New Zealand. One day I asked Bill how his parents had fostered his intellectual development. He said that, though they had not attended college, they had wanted him to excel academically and had encouraged him by buying him a book every week.

Though I was a divorced mother at the time, I took the girls to a bookstore each Friday and bought each a paperback of her choice. (Of course, I guided their selections.) When I eventually could no longer afford this practice, we visited the library frequently and subscribed to excellent children's magazines, such as *Highlights* and *Cricket*.

But all of this takes *time*. Family time. Personal time. If parents rush in at 6:00 P.M., tired and hungry, and the children are waiting with clamorous needs, it is unlikely the family will linger at dinner for a leisurely time of reading aloud. Besides who will have had the presence of mind to find the book? Life needs to be peaceful and orderly to do something as simple as read aloud each evening.

Thus, on-site, interested mothers oversee their children's intellectual development, offer help with homework, and give the child the message that he has interested, involved parents. This is important if children are to achieve academically. Studies of maternal employment generally find that sons of employed mothers perform less well academically than sons of full-time mothers. Why is this so? Boys may need more guidance and supervision than their "time-poor" working mothers provide. Psychologist Ann Crouter and her colleagues write that to achieve academically a child needs "an effective monitor" who knows about his day and is aware of his experiences.[13]

Some parents are not satisfied with educating their children informally. Untold families are engaged in home-schooling their children to foster creativity, independence, and academic success. One family in California has received national press attention for their efforts. David and Micki Colfax have been so successful in teaching their children at home that their three oldest sons—Grant, Drew, and Reed—got into Harvard.[14] Encouraging their children to assume responsibility and learn independence, David and Micki fostered each child's intellectual interests. The parents guided their children's reading, provided a large library at home, and encouraged them to use the public library. They helped their children take their interests and run with them. Said Drew, who built his own telescope, "If we had any sort of interest, if we didn't already have the materials we would get them."[15]

Disciplining Our Children

More is involved in a child's development, however, than just intellectual stimulation. To learn to live most effectively, a child must become a disciplined human. He learns as his parents endlessly, patiently teach him the rudiments of self-discipline and as they model disciplined lives before him.

Although children need to be disciplined by their fathers, the mother at home is a primary source of discipline for her children. She is on-site, so she's elected to control her children's behavior. If she doesn't, her life will be chaotic. Who can wait until daddy comes home when Junior decorates the walls of the family room with his new magic markers? Mom is in charge, whether she wants to be or not. If she does a good job, the reward is a well-behaved child who likes himself and is well-liked by others. If she doesn't, she will create a hellion who is unpopular with his peers and who will have a hard time controlling his impulses as an adolescent, giving his parents grief.

When a parent fails to control his child's behavior, this

signifies that the parent has minimal investment in parenting and is putting his energies elsewhere.[16] Poorly disciplined children don't believe their parents are committed to them and most feel unloved. I have a friend, a lawyer educated at Dartmouth, who was turned over to babysitters to rear while his mother played golf and his father poured his time into a successful medical practice. "I never really felt my parents loved me," said Zachery. "They seldom disciplined me for *anything.* I was just an ornament in their middle-aged lives."

It takes time and energy to love and discipline our children. I had no idea when my babies were born just how many hours I would spend in the next eighteen years shaping their behavior. Yet what better person than their mother to teach them to speak to adults with respect, to care for their pets responsibly, to clean their rooms, to handle their angry feelings, to develop good study habits, to obey curfews, to show compassion? So most of the time, especially in their early years, that someone was me. Don helped with the discipline on evenings and weekends, and his presence was even more critical when the girls became teenagers.

Teaching Values

Have you ever wondered why some children have the same values as their parents while others rebel and become diametrically opposed to everything their parents hold dear? Psychologists have found this doesn't happen by chance.

Psychologist Kevin MacDonald says children who have a warm, affectionate relationship with their parents will adopt their parents' values, while those who have grown up in conflict-ridden homes subject to a daily barrage of negativism will not.[17] Yet when children and adolescents reject their parents' values they are at risk for behavior problems later on. Adrift, alienated, these young people tend to be isolated as well.

This becomes strategic when our children begin to walk the high school corridors with adult bodies and raging hormones. Gone is the adoring daughter of the latency period; gone the dutiful, quietly obedient son. Instead our adolescent sons and daughters are often mercurial, difficult, intractable.

Norman Kiell suggests adolescence is a psychological state "as definitely characterized by domestic explosions and rebellions as typhoid is marked by fevers."[18] And while the hormones in adolescent children rage, parents are themselves prey to midlife angst. At the same time an adolescent is struggling with his identity, his parents are confronting their mortality and renegotiating their marriages. This often creates a volatile mix.

Yet what our teenagers need is for us to hold the line, recognizing that while adolescence is a time of turbulence, it is also the time when identity is forged. Psychoanalyst Erik Erikson wrote in *Childhood and Society* that adolescence is a psychosocial stage when adolescents are involved in a difficult identity crisis. Erikson believed that creating a sense of identity was so difficult that most adolescents exhibited some degree of psychopathology.[19]

Adolescent Depression

What are the adolescents' struggles? Self-esteem precipitously drops at age twelve and slowly begins an upward climb, reaching some kind of stability at age eighteen.[20] While children from strong, intact homes seem to handle the stresses of adolescence with a minimum of turmoil, many adolescents struggle with some degree of depression.

One 1990 study examined Canadian high school students and found that about a third experienced mild to clinical depression. This is "an extremely high figure that illustrates the seriousness of the problem."[21]

Some psychologists believe ideas about suicide are common during adolescence. The teenager often feels inferior, he struggles with identity, he may be jealous of siblings, and he is separating from his parents. One study of 407 high school students found that 32 percent of the males and 46 percent of the females had thought of taking their own lives. And the females in this study reported more emotional problems, lower self-esteem, and less parental support than did the males.[22]

As noted at the beginning of this chapter, suicide is on the rise among young people. Psychiatrist Larry Brain, director of Child and Adolescent Services at the Washington, D.C., Psychiatric Institute, believes adolescents today have greater stress to deal with than adolescents of an earlier era. As proof he cites the changing family structure, dual career marriages, divorce, and lack of extended family.[23] Consequently, many young people today feel alienated and detached from their families as well as society.

Which adolescents are at risk for suicide? Those who have lost parents early in life (due to death or divorce), those who have no strong inner core or sense of self, those who are frightened by life, and those who were maternally deprived are particularly vulnerable. These teenagers may become walking time bombs. Also, adolescents with perfectionistic parents whose standards are impossible to meet are at risk. Some adolescents snap under the strain, feeling they must get A's in every academic subject to please their demanding parents. Others who are at risk include loners who feel empty inside, substance abusers, and those who are accident prone.[24]

At-risk teenagers come from families that have severe marital conflict. Their fathers are usually absent or ineffectual. Moreover, one or both parents may be alcoholics who utterly fail to meet the child's need for emotional support.[25]

Given that adolescence is generally a stressful, confusing time, this is no time for mom and dad to retreat and retrench. It is also not a time for mom to be so involved in her career she has too little time and energy to stay the course. If we either cave in to our adolescents' demands or absent ourselves from their lives, we force our kids to seek guidance from their peer group. As one high school teacher says, "I don't believe kids turn to their peers because they are close to them or even because they like them that much. Sometimes they go to their peers by default. Nobody's home."

What is needed is a strong parental coalition which can stand firm in the face of adolescent misbehavior. This is hard to provide since parents, who have been "dethroned" by their teenagers, are bombarded daily by their adolescents' fluctuating mood states. Yet a united front is essential.[26]

We cannot give up even if some days we want to. Especially then our children need an emotionally available mother to hold onto the reins. Though we give our older children greater slack, we still need to know where they are after school, who they're with, and when they will return home. Said one mother, "I believe in giving my son some freedom, then if he handles that responsibly, I give him some more. You can't be rigid and authoritarian with teenagers." This mother is also an involved parent who knows what her kids are doing after school. She is not out "doing her own thing." Kids do not profit from parental absenteeism and neglect, and the empty house can become a dangerous place.

Parents are naive if they assume their teenagers will never use the empty house for drugs or afternoon sex. Remember the divorced mother in the movie *Parents*? Conned by the wild thumps of her daughter's heavy metal music, this mom wises up when the local photo-processor mistakenly swaps her daughter's Kodak-recorded coitus for her bank promotion photos.

Having observed adolescents and listened to them talk over the years, I know many find empty houses a convenient place to engage in self-destructive behavior. Consequently, I made sure I was home most afternoons. Did I distrust my daughters? Once a teenager myself, I remember how seductive and intense peer pressure can be. I did not know then what psychologists have discovered—that parents, not peers, are the primary moral influence for their teens. Had I known this, I would still have made it a practice to be home when the girls were present.

Not that either girl always appreciated my presence. I remember once when Kristen was in the tenth grade and using her abundant energies to gain popularity, she said in a snippy voice, "Why don't you go to work full-time? Most of my friends' mothers work."

I looked at her and grinned, "Oh, I see. You don't like having me at home, keeping track of your comings and goings."

"Right!" she said, smiling.

"But you need me here, whether you know it or not," I retorted.

And so I manned the fort, even after I returned to graduate school. I simply planned my schedule around the girls' after-school activities. This paid off in spades when Kristen became a senior and went through a period of turmoil with several of her friends. For weeks she and they were estranged, and I, who had earlier been a pariah, became a valued support player. Often when she came home from school during that period, Kris needed me to apply first aid to her wounded ego.

During her freshman year in college, Kris said to me, "Mom, I'm glad you were home during that time. I really needed you. I hated it on those rare days when I would drive up the driveway and your car was gone. If you hadn't been there for me, I don't know what I would have done."

As they grow older, children will need less of mother's time and energy. Once her children are in school all day, a woman has free hours to use in a meaningful capacity. Some women go back to school, some work part-time outside the home, others begin a home-based business.

CEOs in the Suburbs

The amount of contact parents have with
their children has dropped 40 percent
during the last quarter-century.
William R. Mattox, Jr.

At one time Sarah Edwards was a harried working mother. According to Sarah, "Juggling a successful career and motherhood meant being dead tired most of the time and not being able to do either job with the dedication I wanted."[1]

One day, however, Sarah went to see two consultants she had worked with as a government administrator. Both were successfully operating home-based businesses. When Sarah left them, she told herself, "This is for me."[2]

It took Sarah several years before she was finally able to work at home. Only after training to become a psychotherapist did she finally start a private practice at home as a clinician. Sarah says, "Working at home was like having flowers delivered to me every day."[3] Not only did Sarah become a healthier, happier woman, but she became a more relaxed mother.

Sarah's husband Paul soon joined her at home, starting his own business as a political consultant. Today these husband-wife entrepreneurs are contributing editors and columnists for *Home Office Computing* magazine, cohosts of the weekly "Home Office" show on the Business Radio Network as well as the Los Angeles radio show, "Here's to Your Success." Sarah and Paul Edwards have also written a book titled *Working from Home* which is a must for anyone desiring to start a home-based business.

The Movement Toward Home

Sarah and Paul Edwards are part of the "electronic cottage" movement Alvin Toffler forecast in his 1980 book *The Third Wave.* Futurist Toffler predicted that increasing numbers of men and women would tire of long and expensive commuting and elect to work from home. According to Toffler, when the cost of installing and operating home telecommunications falls below the cost of commuting, a great upsurge in the number of home-based workers will occur. Toffler rightly noted that in 1980 many men and women already worked from home, among them lawyers, designers, secretaries, therapists, architects, music teachers, salesmen, and insurance agents.[4]

Why did Toffler write a decade ago that America would move toward a "home-centered society?" Noting that the nuclear family was in trouble, he predicted people would shift their work place from city to home as a way of strengthening the family. Said Toffler, "Work at home suggests a deepening of face to face and emotional relationships in both the home and neighborhood."[5]

Aware of this, women increasingly are leaving the marketplace to work at home. These are the new CEOs of the suburbs. The U.S. Census Bureau reported in 1987 that some 2.9 million women owned their own businesses.[6] Of these, slightly more than half were home-based. Who worked at home? While many of these women entrepreneurs had only a high school education, roughly two-thirds took business courses or attended seminars to increase their knowledge. Most started their businesses with little or no capital, borrowing from banks or families or using savings accounts for start-up cash.

Why Work at Home?

Why are greater numbers of women electing to work at home? According to Marion Behr and Wendy Lazar, authors of *Women Working at Home*, the reasons are obvious: proximity to children, the desire to avoid commuting, the need for additional income, flexibility, and the low cost of operating a home-based business.[7] Possibly the greatest reward of working at home is that "home is where the kids are." What mother hasn't felt anguish when she has had to drop an ill or unhappy child off at day care?

Listen to one mother's unhappiness as she struggles with her absence from her children's lives: "I have a B.S. degree in home and family services and work for the juvenile court. I see what happens to so many kids who do not get the attention they need. I have always been opposed to working outside the home, but feel trapped because I have not been able to come up with a workable alternative."

This mother of two preschoolers is afraid of what the future holds if she doesn't come home to nurture her children, but she has no idea of how to translate her skills and education into a marketable at-home career. What, she asks, is she to do?

How well I remember those feelings. Moving to Seattle after two years in London, I needed money to supplement the monthly child support. So I determined to find the perfect part-time job that would mesh with my education and skills while allowing me to be home half days. I found nothing that interested me. At the height of my frustration, when I had begun to wonder if I would have to work full-time, a friend called. Jim Leach was then the director of the Washington State Criminal Justice Education and Training Center.

"Have you ever written a newsletter or quarterly journal?" asked Jim, after hearing that I still hadn't found a job.

"No," I said. "But I did teach college kids to write, so I know I could produce the articles."

"What about working with a printer?" he asked. "Do you know anything about layout?"

"No," I said hesitantly. "But I'm sure I could learn."

Within a few days I had agreed to produce a quarterly journal for the Criminal Justice Education and Training Center, applied for a business license, ordered business cards and stationary, and decided on an hourly fee. My editorial consulting firm was launched.

I worked at the Justice Center for a few hours each week, obtaining my assignments, conferring with Jim. Then I scheduled interviews with lawyers and judges or worked at home writing articles. This schedule worked well. The hours spent at the center or in interviews gave me essential adult contact, and the hours at home provided the necessary solitude for creative work.

Best of all, I could be with Holly and Kristen before and after school. I dropped them off at their schools each morning. Though Kris spent a couple of hours each day at the local day care center after morning kindergarten, I picked her up at 2:00 and we had the rest of the afternoon together—time for shopping, outings, friends, activities. My children have many happy memories from those years I worked at home. Both say those were the happiest years of their childhood.

The mother who works from home has the opportunity to spend quality afternoons with her children. Cherie Fuller, a freelance writer, left her job as a teacher to pursue her writing at home. She says, "I've never regretted that decision. With my new flexibility, I can watch Chris's 3:30 basketball games, pick Alison up from school, and be home when one of them is sick. I do have trying times when deadlines stack up like piles of laundry, and it's my day to volunteer at school. But overall, I'm delighted with my arrangement."[8]

Lest one think working at home is a second-rate way to go, here are some famous companies that got their start at home: Apple Computer, Baskin-Robbins Ice Cream, Domino's Pizza, Ford Motor Company, Hallmark Cards, Mrs. Field's Cookies, Nike, *Reader's Digest*, and Hewlett-Packard, to name a few.[9]

One woman who started her business in her basement flat and lived to see her shops open in such cities as Milan, New York, Tokyo, London, and Melbourne was Laura Ashley. A mother at home, Laura initially began by printing designs on fabric, which was later made into towels and sold in London shops. Although the business started slowly in 1953, Laura Ashley's papers and fabrics are highly prized by women throughout the world.[10] So a woman has no idea how far her talents will take her when she begins to turn her gifts into profit from home.

Where to Begin?

You may be thinking, "I'm convinced, but where do I begin? How do I translate my skills into profit?" Though an in-depth response is beyond this chapter's scope, I hope to provide you with a plan for proceeding.

First, ask yourself the following:

- What do I enjoy doing?

- What do others identify as my skills and talents?

- What are my hidden talents?

- Do I have the personality characteristics needed for working at home?

For the moment, disregard that censorious voice that says, "Oh, you can't do that," or "You'd never make any money at that." If you're like me, your inner censor can kill creativity, so you must quietly and firmly turn it off. As a high school English teacher preparing students to write essays, I often said, "When you're anxious or your mind is blank, just write down everything that comes to mind. Do some brainstorming. Then group the ideas together logically."

Once you sit down with pen and paper and write down what comes to mind, you will begin to get in touch with inner desires as well as perceptions about your abilities. A friend told me that as she approached forty, she felt a need to dream a new dream. So she sat on the beach one day and asked herself: What do I really want to do with my life? As she watched the breaking waves, she realized she desired to become an accountant, working from home. Since she hadn't finished college, she knew she'd have to go back to school to achieve her goal. With her two children in school all day, this women determined to complete her education and acquire the essential credentials so she could start her own home-based business.

Next, think about the skills and talents your friends praise and actually utilize. Can any of these be parlayed into a new career at home? Jane Dull began her business in interior decoration when her friends started asking her to help them organize and decorate their homes. "I always loved interior design," says Jane, "but my father wanted me to become a teacher instead." Yet, even as she prepared to become a teacher, Jane took all of her college electives in interior design.

About a year ago a friend asked Jane to help her choose "everything" for a new home. Jane says, "I did it just for fun, but then another friend hired me to redo her house. I loved it. It was a ball, and I got paid for it."

This was the impetus Jane needed to start her own home-based business in interior design. Her activities span the gamut of creating plans to sewing fabric for cornices. And Jane works as her schedule permits. She uses little child care, consulting on evenings or weekends when her husband can babysit. As a mother of five children ranging in age from four to seventeen, Jane likes her job's flexibility. Even when she spends time with her family (her first priority) rather than pursuing clients, Jane finds that "every time we need the money, something falls in my lap."

After assessing your skills and interests, it is time for a moment of truth. Do you have the personality characteristics needed for successful home-working? Are you motivated? Can you plan your time and execute a project, meeting deadlines? Do you enjoy working alone?

Susan once managed a large office with thirty employees before her baby Carlin was born. Now she works in public relations from home and loves it. "My former job was so stressful," says Susan. "Now I find myself relishing the freedom to set my own schedule and spend time with my baby."

On the other hand, Marietta, who enjoys the social contacts

that work outside the home provides, found working at home lonely. For a time she tried working at home for her former boss, but decided she'd rather go to the office for two days each week. "When I am at work, I work and socialize," says Marietta, "and when I'm home I throttle back to live a relaxed lifestyle, caring for my daughter, meeting friends for lunch." Obviously, home-based businesses are not for everyone.

As Sarah and Paul Edwards put it, working at home means "more control over your schedule and your environment than ever before. You are in charge, there is no boss standing over your shoulder. There is no time clock to punch, no bell to tell you when to start and when to stop. There is no procedures manual for working at home—it's up to you. It can be a dream come true or a nightmare, depending on what you do. It's 100 percent up to you!"[11]

People who flourish working at home are those who can create their own structure, who can set and achieve goals, and who are highly motivated to succeed.[12]

Next, find out all you can about your area of interest and about how to turn your interests into profit. As you read books and magazine articles about working at home, you will form a plan you feel comfortable with. Read local library notice boards for listings of seminars and workshops for beginning entrepreneurs. One mother who heads a successful home-based advertising agency says she learned valuable information about self-management and marketing from seminars she attended.

If your library is limited, search book stores for books such as *Homemade Money* by Barbara Brabec and *Working at Home* by Lindsay O'Connor. The following recent publications deal with working at home: Lynie Ardent's *The Work at Home Sourcebook*, Norman Schreibei's *Your Home Office* and *Start, Run and Profit from Your Own Home-Based Business* by Gregory and Patricia Kishel. These books contain chapters on establishing a home office, pricing and marketing your skills, services, or products. An excellent reference book is a must for the beginning entrepreneur.

Begin networking. Canvass friends and family acquaintances to find other mothers working at home in your area of interest or expertise. Have these women over for lunch or take them out for dessert and coffee. I have learned an enormous amount from talking to such women on the phone—women who meet deadlines, care for their children, and are willing to share their expertise with me. Whenever I've started a new venture, I've searched for a role model, someone who is already doing successfully what I want to do. Often this role model will give me access to her network.

Women in the workplace know the value of networking and women who work out of their homes should, too. Networking not only provides emotional support, but saves valuable time. In my area, contacts with other writers have helped me learn about literary agents, writers' conferences, advances, editors, and marketing articles. I recently put a friend in touch with the editor of a national magazine I had worked for. She, in turn, gave me contacts at a national newspaper and a summer writers' conference.

Writer Georganne Fiumara, who has published in national magazines such as *Family Circle*, recognized the value of networking. She founded the Mothers' Home Business Network and publishes a New York-based quarterly publication by that name to help women network nationally.

Now create a work space or set up an office, and learn about legal matters from securing a business license to finding out about your city or county's zoning ordinances. According to Cherie Fuller, the U.S. Small Business Administration has local chapters that provide such information, as well as a free business start-up kit and counseling services.[13] Since eighteen states have laws governing work from home, Sarah and Paul Edwards suggest seeking legal assistance in establishing a small business.[14] These are essential matters that need to be settled before you send out a press release or tell your community that you are in business.

Realize that the hardest task you may have is self-management. Writer Ann Hibbard, who has two school-age children, plays tennis regularly, and is heavily involved in her church, says one "has to be an extremely disciplined person to write at home." Hibbard, whose first book is *Family Celebrations*, admits she "goes in and out of discipline. Sometimes I'm totally disciplined and sometimes I fritter my time away."

Any mother who works from her home has to create a schedule that works for her. Some women find this easy; others impossible. If a woman is to succeed at home-work, she not only has to create a workable schedule, but she needs to maintain it. But what if children get sick or stay home on snow days? Sometimes this means working late nights, early mornings, or weekends to meet deadlines. Those I've interviewed who are happiest working at home are those who have the greatest flexibility in their schedules. In most cases, however, these mothers were earning less than those who have carved out more regular hours and who have rigid deadlines to meet (and who hire child care when needed).

The Pay-off

Finally, what are the rewards of working at home? Most mothers who have successfully launched home-based businesses feel they have the best of both worlds. They can be mothers first, adapting their work to their children's needs, but be entrepreneurs as well. "It's good to be home with my son," says Lisa Greenfield. "I feel I know more about his needs than anyone else. I couldn't have left him to go to work when he was small."

While Lisa can spend valuable hours with her small son, she also has the good feelings gained from managing a successful advertising agency, working for such clients as the American Red Cross and *Best Weddings*. Before her son was born, Lisa worked as the art director for an ad agency and supervised five designers. When she decided to leave her job, she took her skills and contacts with her. In working for projects for both Fortune 500 companies and small businesses, Lisa subcontracts some of her work to other designers and marketers.

Writer Nancy Pearcey loves working at home because of the intellectual stimulation it provides. Becoming pregnant when she was a seminary student, Nancy, who has published in *The Human Life Review* and *The World and I*, began her writing career producing science readers for elementary school children. Nancy has worked at home now for thirteen years, until recently earning a third of the family income. Now writing her first book, Nancy says her work satisfies an "intellectual hunger" since in writing she is not "just taking in but is also giving out—a rich experience."

Working at home allows a woman to be available to her children most hours and to provide additional family income. It also gives her life a depth and richness it might

Possibilities for a Home-based Business

———— •꞊◦◖◗◦꞊• ————

Accounting service
Advertising agency
Aerobics classes
Answering service
Architectural designer
Art instruction
Babysitting referral service
Balloon decoration
Bartering service
Bed and breakfast inn
Cake decorating
Calligraphy
Career counseling
Catering
Cleaning services
Color consulting
Computer programming or
    tutoring
Dancing instruction
Data processing service
Desktop publishing services
Editorial services
Fashion consultant
Financial consulting
Gift buying service
Gourmet cooking school
Graphic designer
Interior design services

Job placement and referral
    service
Landscape designer
Literary agent
Management consultant
Marketing consultant
Music instruction
Needlepoint instruction
Personnel consultant
Pet sitting for unusual ani-
    mals
Photography
Public relations service
Quilting
Resume writing service
Shopping services
Singing telegram service
Tax preparation
Technical writer
Toymaking
Tutoring
Wardrobe consulting
Word processing/secretarial
    services
Writing newsletters and
    trade publications

(Taken from *Working from Home* by Sarah and Paul Edwards.)

otherwise lack. This is not to say working at home doesn't have its crazy moments or humorous asides. One mother was in her basement office talking to a client when her two-year-old started screaming from the top of the basement stairs. The mother began stammering as she struggled to focus on her client's needs and block out the toddler's persistent shrieks. Supposedly in the care of his older sister, the toddler continuously banged the door, yelling "*Mommeee.*" Finally, the client could stand it no longer and asked, "Do you have your office in a day care center?" This is only one problem the home-based entrepreneur faces. Another is to monitor the hours her child is in the care of others while mom works at home.

If a woman is staying home to be accessible to her children and then spends most of her child's waking hours in her office (or finds that her emotional well is empty), she needs to question what she's doing. It is not enough simply to be present in the home if a sitter is providing most of the child care or the parent is emotionally inaccessible.

To provide "good enough mothering," a woman needs to manage her time, her self, her moods: Moreover, she needs to take the longer view of her life and understand she is only home for a season.

PART TWO

Home for a Season

I grow lives. Sometimes as a writer;
always as a mother. And I grow my own.
Sherry von Ohlsen

When my children were very young, some days I felt they would never grow up. At the end of a wearying day of changing a dozen diapers, attending to unhappy cries, and engaging in baby talk, I was convinced my brain was slowly and irrevocably atrophying. I wasn't merely losing a few brain cells, mind you; I was teetering on the brink of mental retardation. I wondered wistfully if I would ever again be able to go into the bathroom without a baby crawling after me, or leave the house without slinging Kristen on one hip, trailing little Holly by the hand, and wrestling with a bulging diaper bag.

Knowing little about the developmental stages of a woman's life, it never occurred to me to reflect on the panoramic sweep of a woman's existence, start to finish. Had I done so, I might have realized the years of childrearing were only one rich, valuable portion of my life span—a season to be cherished and enjoyed.

Now my daughters are grown. They have even become people I like and enjoy. We often go out for coffee or sit in the living room, having stimulating conversations that go on for hours about psychology, literature, and life. I now can spend all day alone in the bathroom if I want to (though my husband would find this peculiar). And when I leave my house, sometimes I carry nothing more than a svelte, black handbag.

Where did the years of childrearing go?

The years, like the seasons, have come and gone. In a few short months I will celebrate my fiftieth birthday. When I was twenty-eight, I never imagined I would some-day be fifty. I guess fifty just sounded so old. Ironically, I won't be surprised if I actually feel younger in my fifties than I did in my forties when I worked on my doctorate and mothered two sometimes difficult teenagers.

From this vantage point in the life cycle, I have learned some valuable truths. First, don't wish any of the years of your life away. They will slip away soon enough. Second, enjoy life as it comes, for our experiences and our rela-tionships will never be the same again. The hard times, if mined for their valuable lessons, can illumine the rest of our days.

Let's reflect for a moment on the seasons of a woman's life and determine how you can find the fruitful summer season of childrearing rich and rewarding, a time in which you feel fulfilled and are able to give your children the nurture they need.

The Seasons of Female Development

To date, psychologists have failed to conceptualize a the-ory of normal female development. When they have done developmental studies, they have studied only men and extrapolated from these results to women.[1]

Even Erik Erikson, who wrote about the eight psychosocial stages of development, was writing about men and had little to say about women's development. When he did speak of women, it was to say a woman's identity could only be found after she chose a mate. In Erikson's model, while men forge an identity in adolescence and then seek heterosexual intimacy in young adulthood, women seek intimacy and, in so doing, find their identity. Women's identities are embedded in their relationships.[2] The implication is that men know who they are before women do.

In *Finding Herself* Ruth Josselson says that the "most important task facing women today is the formation of identity, for it is in the realm of identity that a woman bases her sense of herself as well as her vision for the structure of her life."[3] What does Josselson mean by *identity*? This term includes a woman's choices, principles, and the priorities she establishes for her life—a stable sense of self.

Josselson began a study in 1971 on women's development of identity. Initially, she conducted interviews with sixty college seniors; twelve years later, she again interviewed thirty-four of these same women.

She found that while separation-individuation is a key theme for men in establishing an identity, women are more concerned about staying connected to the key players in their lives. For one thing, women never completely separate from their mothers. The relationship a daughter has with her mother is intense and lifelong. Josselson says, "Separation between mothers and their daughters then is only partial; at some level they always remain bound up with each other as though neither ever quite sees herself as a fully separate person."[4]

Josselson found that identity for the women in her study was not tied to the political or occupational issues, but rather to social and religious realities. Also, she found that daughters internalize the core values and priorities of their mothers and either accept them or fight against them.

According to Josselson, "the internal presence of mother, her wishes and her approving smile, hovers just at the corner of consciousness, an ever-present other to whom a woman is continually responding."[5] Josselson believes that every woman must somehow integrate something of her mother's values and priorities into her own life or risk identity diffusion. To totally reject mother is to never quite know who one is. Says Josselson: "Some aspect of mother must be mixed in the identity in order to bind it, to make it cohere."[6]

In this study, 85 percent of the women were close to their mothers ten years after graduating from college, and 50 percent said their mothers were either their closest or second closest connection. (Only 48 percent remained close to their fathers, and only two women said dad was either the closest or second closest person in their world.) Josselson writes that many will find this data surprising since the post-feminist woman is supposed to have left her mother "in the dust."

I remember the discomfort and anxiety I felt years ago when I read in a popular magazine that daughters reject their mothers as role models if mom stays home. At the time my children were in high school struggling with their identity, and some days it felt like they were rejecting me. I wondered if they had any idea of the financial sacrifices Don and I were making so that I could be home and available to them.

In intervening years, I have found this message to be false. Each of my daughters has identified with me to some extent. Holly, who shares my love of literature and writing, was an English major and published short stories while in college. And Kristen, a psychology major, is now applying to graduate programs in clinical psychology. Both daughters have become almost colleagues. Holly has edited my writing and Kristen discusses psychological findings with me. So I was not, as a mother at home developing her gifts, rejected as a role model. This is supported by Josselson's finding that even when the women in her study worked, they still identified with their traditional mother's commitment to nurturance and family.

Identity and Confusion

The women in Josselson's study anchored their lives and identities in relationships. Many were disillusioned by less-than-satisfying careers. For these women in their early thirties, even those who were employed, identity was based on connections rather than career. Josselson has found this true in her clinical practice as well. She has treated highly successful professionals for up to two years in intensive psychotherapy and found they talk about their relationships rather than their work. "Work success," says Josselson, "does not compensate for unfulfilled needs for human relatedness."[7]

Josselson's perceptions are supported by Harvard psychologist Carol Gilligan, who found that achieving women do not describe themselves by their work but rather by their relationships. "If anything," says Gilligan, "they regard their professional activities as jeopardizing their own sense of themselves, and the conflict they encounter between achievement and care leaves them divided in judgment or feeling betrayed."[8]

This was underscored for me recently when I received a letter from a woman who is a corporate executive. Childless at forty, she writes: "My life today is the 'glamorous' life that is pushed on many American women. I work for a large firm, have an impressive title, and share responsibility for a staff of a hundred people at the V.P. level. I am grateful for all the opportunities that have been given me, but I am also aware there is little real glamour in my work, and *I have missed much that mothers have experienced.*"

Making the Most of Summer

With this in mind, how can a mother at home maximize those years when she is marrying and rearing children— the summer of her life? What positive steps can she take to create a life that nourishes both herself and her family? How can she ensure that she will be able to provide the emotional support her children need?

Each of us has been given gifts to develop and share with the world around us. It is not important whether our gifts are major or minor. What matters is how diligent we are in cultivating what we have been given.

We need to discover and value our gifts—whatever they are.

Introduced to an admiral's wife once, I asked her what she enjoyed doing. She replied, "silly little things—needlepoint and gardening." I felt sad this gracious, southern woman denigrated those activities that obviously gave her pleasure. Not all of us have culturally rewarded gifts like singing, acting, writing, and painting. But we can enrich our world nonetheless.

Barbara Beckett is open about enjoying the various

aspects of life at her home in Ohio. Recently she gave up her part-time job to return home full-time, a place she's "always cherished and found very, very rewarding." Barbara loves to chat with her friends and family, do needlework, can food, garden, cook and bake. But most of all, she loves entertaining friends. In addition, Barbara takes the time to decorate notecards with flowers made from embroidery thread. She also wrote a little poem that pithily describes the mother-at-home's situation:

Housewife/Mother of Two

Some say I've lost my mind and others think I'm crazy!

While some suggest I stay at home because I'm lazy!

I'm happy to tell them, "This is most untrue."

I just changed my career when I answered the ad . . .

Wanted: Housewife/Mother of two.

Dare to Pursue Your Interests

One of the little acknowledged secrets of life is that a woman's gifts can flourish during her years at home. Whether she is potter, karate champ, aerobics fanatic, gardener, neighborhood psychologist, budding politician, or artist, the mother at home has the opportunity to expand her horizons, take a talent, and run with it. As a corporate executive has said, "Anyone who works forty or sixty plus hours per week and commutes, has little time, after functioning as husband and father, to pursue his own interests." The woman at home has that privilege. Granted, she has little time available when her kids are small and constantly demanding, but once they are in school, she will find she has a few hours each week to think her own thoughts and begin to dream her own dreams again. And as she uses the time, capitalizing on the opportunities that come her way, she will develop abilities and interests she never imagined possible.

Eleanor Carr feels she has grown as a person by using her gifts during her years at home. When her sons Peter and Jim were in nursery school, Eleanor taught at the School for Wee Learners nine hours per week so her boys could attend free. "This helped me meet new people," says Eleanor, "and it helped me value mothering more highly." As the boys grew and Eleanor became a den mother, she discovered she was "handy with tools." Eleanor eventually took classes in upholstery, and during the years when she and her husband couldn't afford new furniture, she reupholstered her second-hand items like a professional.

When her daughter Julie was eleven, Eleanor traded her hat as den mother for Girl Scout leader, discovering she had considerable gifts as an organizer and administrator. It took some fancy headwork to plan all those weekend cookouts for Julie's hungry troop. After her stint in Girl Scouts, Eleanor then became an organizer in her church and was tapped frequently to serve on various committees.

Eleanor attributes her increased self-esteem to all her years of helping others. As other adults praised her for her competence and dependability, she became more extroverted and confident.

In time Eleanor grew concerned about poverty and homelessness. When her children were teenagers, it was a natural next step for her to work at Bethany Women's

Shelter in Washington, D.C. There Eleanor, an upper middle-class, suburban woman, sometimes cooked for homeless women. Years later she became interim director of Bethany House and served on their Board of Directors.

Eleanor has a heart for homeless women. This wife and mother who jokes about perpetually charbroiling her family's food has not only cooked for Bethany House, but she has on occasion bathed homeless women. "I realized these women are just like me," says Eleanor. "Although many are mentally ill, they have families. Some, at one time, had careers. All have their hurts. Most people view the homeless with fear, but that's because they don't realize the homeless are just like us in many respects."

In Eleanor's work with the homeless, she has also ventured into the drug underworld. A deeply religious woman, Eleanor has gone into a crack house looking for the young woman who often calls her for help in the middle of the night. "It felt strange," says Eleanor, "going into a dark basement room with a D.C. police car sitting outside. But I wasn't afraid. I felt God was with me."

Eleanor believes her years of volunteering have greatly enriched her life. "You start out doing one little thing," she says, "and over time you realize how much more you have to offer. People are appreciative of what you give."

Jane Dull is another mother at home who has an unusual gift for home organization. Jane admits she has been a "neatnick" since adolescence. While most parents fail to get their teenagers to keep their rooms clean, Jane used to shake her chenille scatter rugs and walk *around* them so she wouldn't leave any visible footprints.

Having five active children, however, has cured Jane of that compulsive behavior. Nevertheless, this woman who lives by the rule, "Don't put anything away until it's done right," also divides large jobs into small segments and organizes her home one area at a time. She uses masking tape to label her pantry shelves, dumps a drawer a day that gets organized by nightfall, and is currently using her organizational skills to help her friends with their homes.

The Writing Gift

Whether we live in chaos or order matters because our homes reflect something of our personalities. Sherry, once a prowler of flea markets and garage sales, has assembled a Ralph Lauren look for nickels. Sherry has curtains made from Laura Ashley sheets, flea market baskets brimming with towels or magazines, green and red plaid pillows on the white sofa that flanks her stone fireplace. Though she and Carl have struggled financially for years, theirs is one of the loveliest and most original homes I have ever entered. This is, in part, because Sherry is an original. A self-educated woman, Sherry has been developing her considerable gifts at home for years.

Married to Carl, a warm, fun-loving man, Sherry is the mother of two daughters, Erin, thirteen, and Lindsay, eight. Ever since I met Sherry years ago she has wanted to be available to her family, but also to develop her gifts, particularly her writing. It was hard when her girls were young, and Sherry used to say that some years, she only wrote forty-five minutes a day. "That's why it took me five years to write my first novel."

When Lindsay started school, Sherry began to write with a vengeance. She now publishes articles regularly in such publications as *The Christian Science Monitor*. Her last assignment was in Saudi Arabia for *The World and I* magazine—interviewing U.S. troops. Sherry chooses to experience everything she writes about, including soaring and acupuncture, to name a few. She has even been embalmed in mud wraps in her search for the perfect scoop.

How does she find the time? Sherry is a disciplined woman. Her house is tidy when she sits down to write at 8:30 A.M. She takes an hour off at noon for exercise, and then it's back to work until her girls come home and she resumes her role as mother. Each summer Sherry takes a week at a writer's conference to polish her craft. This past year she was asked to be a writing workshop leader and was paid for her expertise.

Sherry says her writing has given her life at home a sense of focus and direction. When she's with her family, she's wholeheartedly present; when she's writing, she is concentrating on her craft. Both give her life richness, depth, texture.

Because we mothers at home have repetitive, sometimes boring and frustrating tasks, we need time each week to develop our gifts. If we paint, we need to find a few hours to set up the easels and uncap the watercolors. If our passion is for gardening, let us plant, hoe, and prune whenever we can. A garden can be a work of art. I tramped around the organic garden of a *Mother Earth News* writer last May and was delighted by what I saw. A wire rabbit run outlined the perimeter. This garden contained mounds of flower areas as well as lettuce, peas, and spinach. Created by a mother who worked with a baby on her back, this garden has been televised on the local evening news!

So make home the studio where you unfurl your canvases, unsheathe your garden shears, and boot up your word processor. Find a room or a corner of a room that is completely yours, a plot of ground for your garden, or an organization to recognize your talents. And lose yourself in a few hours each week in creativity. You will, if you do this diligently, be surprised where your gifts take you—and how they restore your emotional energy.

Home as a Place to Create Memories

Next, a mother needs to think of herself as a scientist and her home as a memory laboratory.

Psychologists have discovered we have different types of memory. Each of us has a short-term memory where we store information for a few seconds or up to a minute. We also have a long-term memory that holds information indefinitely.[9] While the evidence suggests we forget what we take into short-term memory unless the information is passed into the long-term memory, psychologists believe what goes into long-term memory probably stays there throughout life. If we can't remember our childhoods this in no way means these memories have disappeared. It merely means retrieval cues have changed or that we repressed painful memories.

When I was teaching summer school at Georgetown University, my students and I watched a film in which Canadian neurosurgeon Wilder Penfield touched different sections of a woman's brain with a microelectrode. Part of the skull had been removed and the patient's brain lay exposed. Since the brain has no pain receptors, this procedure did not hurt the patient who was fully awake. As the doctor touched different areas of the brain, he asked the patient what she felt, and she responded she was experiencing sensations in different areas of her body. At one point, she began to hear music and hummed a theme from a concert she had attended as a child.

Penfield's research suggests that memories from our

early life are recorded in the brain. While we may have forgotten sights, sounds, and intense personal experiences, nonetheless they are permanently recorded on our magnificent brain. We may hear a song or smell a particular odor and an event will come rushing back.

The famous French writer Marcel Proust dipped a little cake, a madeleine, into a cup of tea and suddenly he remembered his childhood in Combray. The sight and smell of the tea, the shape of the madeleine, released a flood of involuntary memories which he recorded in his classic *Remembrance of Things Past.*

What are the implications of this for the mother at home? I believe this should encourage a woman to consciously work at creating positive, warm memories for her children, memories they can later recall to warm themselves by the fire of remembered joy. This is not to say we will never create unhappy or painful memories for our children. No one can raise a pain-free child; no such humans exist. But we can attempt to interject the positives in our children's lives and to consciously use the occasions of life to produce rich, warm memories.

My earliest memory dates from the years I lived with my grandparents somewhere between the ages of two and five. I remember I was terrified of thunderstorms. When a loud electrical storm raged at the end of a hot, muggy summer day, I would clap my hands over my ears and squeeze my eyes tight.

One day my grandfather, who came in from the pasture smelling of earth and sweat, saw me and scooped me up in his arms. He carried me to the front porch so we could watch the storm together. I can still feel the warm spray of rain on my face, still see the branches tossing wildly in the wind. "Listen to that thunder roll," said Granddaddy, obviously enjoying the moment. "You don't need to be afraid if you're not out there in the storm." That day I felt safe and secure as I watched the raging storm, held in my granddaddy's arms, and I have enjoyed summer storms since.

Whatever sense of security I have is due to times such as these, experienced at my grandparents' farm. Drawing on this storehouse of happy memories, I have consciously tried to create nourishing memories for my children. I have been a companion to them the way my granddaddy was to me, often piling them in the car on summer days for outings. I have talked to them just as my grandparents did to me.

Granddaddy, who dropped out of school in the eighth grade, was quite a story teller. He regaled me for hours with tales of his courtship of Granny. Additionally, Granny, as adept as any social worker, used to probe my inner life. "Now tell me how you feel," she would say about the significant events in my life. People tell me I am a prober par excellence, which simply means I was a good pupil.

Seize the Moment

During our years at home with our children, some events will be more intense than others. People tend to remember moments of emotional intensity, whether positive or negative. That's why some occasions in life seem to say "this moment is memorable." Seize it. Holidays and birthdays are such times. Recently we had a single friend to dinner on her birthday because she said her family never celebrated her birthday growing up. Consequently, she has tried to ignore its significance.

At our house, birthdays are big events. The birthday person dictates the activities that include a party, or at least a family dinner with favorite foods and cake. Also, gift requests are honored, and the other three family members each write a letter, telling the birthday person what he or she means to the writer. I have a small stack of those letters, and in the event of a fire, I'd rush to grab this treasured packet.

"A Place to Be"

Another way to create rich memories for ourselves and our families is to share our homes and lives with others. One's home is not just the private dwelling of a nuclear family; it can also be a place where others find a measure of emotional healing.

A home can be a place of refuge for those who just need to be with a family for a while, as well as for those in emotional pain. One family who ministers beautifully from their home is the Hamiltons. Will and Susie Hamilton met in London twenty years ago when Will was practicing medicine and Susie was a worker for L'Abri Fellowship.

Now living in Fairview, North Carolina, Susie and Will have five children, ranging in age from four to seventeen. Not only does Susie teach all her children art and piano, but both Will and Susie are deeply involved in the life of their small church that used to meet in the renovated garage behind Will's office. Susie has also helped with her father's campaigns for the U.S. Congress, as well as supervised the harvest and sale of twenty-five acres' worth of apples on her parents' nearby farm. In addition, almost since their wedding, Susie and Will have taken in those who show up on their doorstep.

One mountain girl, Rita, lived with Will and Susie for five years. When her father thrust her out of their trailer home, Rita slept beside a cow that first night to keep warm. A minister brought her to Susie's the next day. During the time Rita stayed with the Hamiltons, she helped Susie with household chores, babysat, and attended vocational school until she could support herself. During Rita's stay, I noticed Susie had a peculiar sign attached to the side of her kitchen woodbox: "Don't spit in the woodbox." "What's that for?" I asked Susie, who flipped her blond ponytail and gave an embarrassed smile. "Oh, Rita dips snuff. We would reach in for logs and touch brown goo. Then I finally figured out what it was."

Susie and Will offer their guests *time* with their family. Neither counsels those who come. "If someone is troubled," says Susie, "he usually sees a professional counselor." Instead, they provide a Christian family for others to join, praying for the people who come.

Are there advantages to having a perpetual influx of people? Susie admits she and Will need the labor their guests provide. "We don't really hire people to help us, so those who come have to help out," says Susie. "The boy from Covenant is helping us with our plumbing, and once we had a Swiss hairdresser who gave everybody haircuts."

Susie, who now has a world-wide network of friends, is quick to say it's relatively easy for her to have people live with them since they have the "big house," the parental farm, just up the road. Susie's parents have a thousand-acre working farm that readily absorbs human labor. Also, as part of an open church community, Susie and Will can "plug people into" their laid-back church. She speaks truthfully when she says, "We take care of our loneliness when we reach out to other people." We also add richness to summer's memories, for ourselves, our spouses, our children.

While most of us will not choose to take in people for months or years, we can learn from the Hamiltons. They are role models to the rest of us who live insular lives in suburbia. They teach us that as we give another "a place to be," we are enlarging the boundaries of our own spiritual and emotional selves.

In sum, we are only home for a season. Since our time at home is short, let us make the most of the summer. Then with positive memories we embrace more fully the world beyond our doorstep. We can dance into a winter of rich reward, rather than shuffle into a season of regret.

But what about those mothers who were unnurtured themselves or who feel isolated and alone? They will most likely not have the emotional energy it takes to be creative.

They may feel depleted of energy at the *start* of each day, and the thought of pursuing their dreams or opening their home sounds like a scene from a romance novel.

What do you do if you feel overwhelmed by your life?

Women and Depression

I really do believe that I enjoy hardly
anything on earth while it is present:
Always looking back, or frettingly peering
into the dim beyond.
Edward Lear

Maxine, thirty-three, leans forward, sips from her coffee
cup, and says softly, "I've never been deeply depressed, but
I do have my low hours and days. Sometimes, especially in
the winter when I have been locked in the house all day
with the kids, I feel very low. Then when Tom comes
home, I look at him and say, 'Is this all there is?' "

Stacey, thirty-five, a mother of three small children, is
battling more than a few hours or days of depression. She
has been sliding for several months now, ever since her last
child, a colicky, demanding daughter was born. Stacey, the
child of alcoholic parents, senses her early life is somehow
related to her present vulnerability, but she doesn't quite
know how. Meanwhile, she struggles with a mounting
desire to leave her husband and kids. "I've thought of leaving Charlie before," she says, "but lately I've wanted to run
away from the kids also."

Selena, twenty-nine, and Mike are the parents of one-year-old Cecily. Selena is a computer expert at a northern Virginia corporation. She likes her job but is often exhausted by the multiple demands of her life. She feels she is supposed to manage child, job, marriage, and home effortlessly, but she finds her life becoming increasingly joyless. Mike tells her she is short-tempered most of the time. Standing in front of the refrigerator on sleepless nights, Selena wonders if she is depressed.

Who Gets Depressed?

Depression is something most women struggle with, whether they are employed at home or in the workplace. Obviously, they don't struggle with feelings of depression to the same degree. But sometimes the mother at home believes if she were only back at work, she would be free of the blues. She feels guilty because although she's home, she is not emotionally present for her children. To be effective at home, women need to understand depression: what it is, who gets it, and how to overcome it.

To be human is to be vulnerable to depression. What man or woman alive would say he or she has not, on occasion, felt depressed? To admit this is to join good company, as anyone knows who has read the psalms of David, the lamentations of Job, the laments of Shakespeare's Timon of Athens. Clinicians consider it normal to experience transient feelings of sadness and disappointment from time to time—what some of us call "the blues." What is not normative, and what concerns mental health professionals, is depression that lingers on, permeating the whole cloth of life. When depression is "unduly persistent and pervasive," when it hangs on for several weeks or months, it is considered pathological.[1]

While the majority of Americans will suffer from a serious depression at some time in life, women more than men fall prey to depression. In 1980 Myrna Weissman at Yale, along with her colleague Gerald Klerman, found from extensive study that depression is more common among women than men. This finding persisted whether researchers studied hospitalized patients, outpatients, or participants in community surveys. Women outnumbered the men almost two to one.[2]

Why is this so? Weissman suggests that in women, clinical depression is often in synchrony with the reproductive cycle. We get depressed around the time of menstruation and during postpartum. She also believes that women have a disadvantaged societal position and may suffer from chronically low self-esteem because of feelings of dependency or their "legal and economic helplessness."[3]

While I agree that women are tied to their hormones, I believe we are more vulnerable to depression because we are by nature more relational. As women, we value our relationships highly. Any woman who has ever been involved intimately with a husband or child is a prime target for depression. Demographers have found that mothers, whether married, separated, widowed, or divorced, are particularly depression prone.[4]

In her book *Unfinished Business: Women and Depression*, Maggie Scarf writes that even as babies, females smile more often, are more responsive to the cries of other babies, and pay greater attention to photographs of human faces than do male babies, who at three months still cannot discriminate between photos.[5] We women are not only more sensitive to human faces, but also to touch, taste, and pain. Moreover, we are acutely sensitive to the loss of our significant relationships.

Scarf interviewed Marcia Guttentag, head of the Harvard Project on Women and Mental Health, about a review she did of popular literature. Guttentag found that material geared for a male audience contained themes of adventure, mastery, and triumph, while material directed at women was oriented almost exclusively toward loss. Women were advised about how to handle the loss of lovers, spouses, children, parents, friends: the rupture of their lives' most significant relationships.[6] To care about relationships is to be vulnerable to devastation if they end.

When my first husband left me, I sank into a profound and terrifying depression for the first time in my twenty-eight years. I couldn't sleep. Some nights it was 3:00 A.M. before I drifted into a troubled slumber. In addition, I had difficulty swallowing. All that I could consume was milk, so I rapidly lost ten pounds. I felt desolate and lethargic, as if some part of my body had been dismembered. It was all I could do to get up in the morning, dress and feed my children, and confront the day. The depression lingered on.

I felt undone by the events in my life. I alternated between rage and sadness over the death of my marriage. Mostly, I grieved. My divorce revived all the anguish of my earlier losses.

I felt I needed to be with other people for my sanity—I could not bear lonely days and empty nights. Family lived hundreds of miles away, and having just moved to Connecticut, I had few friends. So I took a job teaching English at a high school.

For nine months I worked, battled despair, and tried to be a good mother with what energy I had left. Employment helped, but did not erase my depression. (Depression has a life of its own; employment is not necessarily a cure.)

In time, the depression lifted. When the three of us moved to London, I stumbled onto a powerful antidote to depression: social support. I developed close friendships with several other women, and through these relationships I found the emotional nurture I needed to heal.

Women need other women. We wither in isolation; we blossom with nourishing friendships. We need our female friends in the good times of life, and we especially need them when we are grappling with the loss of a spouse, parent, or friend.

Lynn is struggling just now with the loss of friendships. She and her husband Noah, a minister, have just moved to a new community for Noah's career advancement. Lynn, who happily agreed to the move, has been surprised at how depressed she has become. "Moving means I have to start all over again," she says. "In Statesville I had friends and a definite role. Here I have nothing important to do."

The American family moves once every five years. Moving can produce powerful feelings of dislocation and transient feelings of depression for women who must redefine themselves, make new friends, and find new outlets for creativity.

In sum, women are more likely to get depressed than men and losses exacerbate depression. This is true because we females look to our relationships to help define us and to maintain a sense of positive self-esteem. When we lose someone we love, when we move and lose good friends, we mourn for a time.

Vulnerability Factors

Some women, however, are more vulnerable to depression than others. Researchers George W. Brown and Tirril

Harris, studying some five hundred women living in London, found that women are vulnerable to depression when they have a lack of intimacy with a husband or lover, have three or more children in the home, or have lost a mother to death prior to age eleven. Nearly half of the depressed women in this study had experienced early maternal death, compared to 17 percent of the nondepressed women in the study. Loss of mother after age eleven or loss of father at any age was unrelated to depression.[7]

Brown and Harris speculate that a mother's death before her daughter is eleven produces an enduring change in the daughter's personality, a change that will generate greater dependency and a decreased sense of self-esteem. Mother-loss gives a girl a lasting sense of insecurity and feelings of incompetence, the feeling that she cannot control the "good things" of her life. The authors of this study argue that before a child is eleven, the mother is in charge of the child's world. So mother's death equals loss of control, something the girl has a hard time recovering from. As a result, she finds later losses intensely threatening.

Brown and Harris found that early maternal loss was also associated with lack of intimacy with a partner. While the researchers believe a confiding relationship with a partner can act as a protective buffer against depression, the depressed mothers in their study lacked such a relationship. It is my conviction that children learn how to speak their innermost thoughts at their mother's knee. If the mother is dead—or emotionally inaccessible for any other reason—her daughter may never have learned to speak the language of the heart.

A woman can learn how to have a confiding relationship

from other women or from a sensitive, open, patient husband. But if a woman has a conflictual relationship with her mother but feels loved by her father, she is often uncomfortable with other women. She has learned male communication skills (rationality, get-to-the-bottom-line argumentation), but she lacks the ability to confide in other women. She does not speak, or listen to, the language of intimate feelings. This woman may simply conclude she doesn't like other women, or that they don't like her. Also, her difficulties with other women may reinforce the negative ideas she holds about womankind, ideas she acquired from her relationship with her mother.

Women and men are fortunate, indeed, if they are taught to speak their feelings, both positive and negative, by a warm, sensitive, accepting mother. This makes men better husbands and women better mothers.

Some of you may say, "My mother and father are still alive. I have experienced no great losses. So why do I struggle with depression?" Our early experiences in our families also have a lot to do with our later vulnerability to depression. Those who come from families short on nurture, guidance, or emotional support are prone to depression later on, while those who grow up in sociable, warm, emotionally close and compassionate families seem to be inoculated against serious depression.

Moreover, loneliness in adolescence and adulthood springs from the same soil as depression. One study found that adolescents who remembered their parents as "emotionally distant, untrustworthy, and hostile" were lonely, while those who remembered their parents as "warm, close and helpful" were not.[8]

In addition, parental rejection in childhood has been linked to later depression. Psychologists Monroe Lefkowitz

and Edward Tesiny studied children when they were eight
years old and again when they were nineteen.[9] They found
maternal rejection was significantly correlated with depression in daughters, and father rejection was even more
powerfully linked with a daughter's later depression.
These researchers suggest that when a daughter fails to
measure up to parental expectations—when parents are
harshly critical or when they withhold affirmation—she
may grow up feeling helpless. These feelings of helplessness later get translated into adolescent and adult depression.

Today Evelyn, the mother of two small sons, looks like a
vulnerable child. Her eyes are sad as she informs me of
her boys' latest shenanigans and finally warms to the reason she stopped by. She wants to talk about her mother.
Evelyn is sorting out her insecurities and wondering why
she is so frantic about winning her mother's love. In the
past she has thought, "If only Mike met my needs, then I
would love myself more."

Evelyn is beginning to understand that an ebb in marital romance is not her most besetting problem. Granted,
Mike has his difficulties communicating from the heart
(he had his own painful early life), but Evelyn's low self-
esteem has deeper roots. "I love my mother," she says, "but
I'm beginning to see that she has little love to give me in
return. Recently I went to see her. She picked up my boys
and hugged them, but when I went up to her and put my
arms around her, she stiffened. That really hurt. Because
my mom has rejected me, I keep expecting others to also
reject me. I'm afraid of losing relationships. I keep trying
to fill up the emptiness inside."

Depression Leads to Black and White Thinking

Depression is feeling inside, "I am unloved; no one will
ever truly love me. Nothing will ever be good." These feelings

are persuasive and powerful. When one is in perpetual darkness, one's will is paralyzed; bleak feelings cloud the emotional landscape. I spoke to a woman who recently emerged from a deep depression that lasted for several months. She feels better now though the previous night she couldn't sleep. "I told myself I had accomplished nothing in my life and I never would do anything significant in the future," says Ellen, an unmarried school teacher.

The woman prone to depression is harsh in her self-evaluations. Where do these perfectionistic thoughts come from? Psychiatrist Robert Leahy, in his book *The Development of the Self*, says the individual who is at risk for later depression forms certain thought patterns early in life that spill over into adulthood.

For example, a woman who experienced parental death or divorce in childhood may think, "No matter what I do, it can all be taken away."[10]

This concept of mental patterns sounds very like John Bowlby's internal working models of attachment. Remember his assertion that we form these attitudes toward ourselves and others early in life? Bowlby also feels that once formed, our internal working models operate outside of our "conscious awareness," and this makes them hard to change. But this is just what we must do to conquer depression.

Overcoming Depression

Cognitive therapy is one form of psychotherapy that addresses the depressed person's negative thought patterns. This was created by Aaron Beck, one of the world's foremost authorities on mood disorders. His cognitive therapy focuses on the way we think. According to one of his protégés, psychiatrist David Burns, Beck's thesis is simple:

We *feel* the way we *think*, and when we are depressed, we think in illogical, self-defeating ways.[11]

In his book *Feeling Good: The New Mood Therapy*, Burns says that when depressives believe life has always been impoverished, they then decide the future will be just as gloomy. "As you look at your past," says Burns, "you will remember all the bad things that have happened to you. As you try to imagine the future, you see only emptiness or unending problems and anguish. This bleak vision creates a sense of hopelessness. This feeling is absolutely illogical, but it seems so real that you are convinced your inadequacy will go on forever."[12]

Our negative thoughts are distorted, says Burns. A depressed person engages in all-or-nothing thinking ("because I failed this exam, I'm stupid"); overgeneralization ("no one will ever like me"); mental filter ("she would reject me if she really knew what I am like"); and labeling ("I'm a loser").

What do we do once we recognize we engage in these distortions? Burns suggests that by writing our automatic thoughts down we can begin to counter the negative, illogical thoughts with rational responses. If a mother punishes her child unfairly and then regrets it afterward, instead of saying, "I'm a bad mother because I spanked Jimmy for something his sister did," she should say, "What I did is unfair, so I'll make amends to Jimmy and try to do better next time."

What about the mother at home who is struggling with the winter blues and a sick, cranky child? Suppose she goes to an office party with her husband only to have an aggressive career woman walk away upon learning the mother stays home. Instead of telling herself the next morning, "What I'm doing here at home isn't valuable," she might say, "So what if *one* unmarried woman spurns me! I know what I'm doing is important."

And the divorced mother who struggles with loss? It is too easy to say, "My husband rejected me; no other man will love me." It's far better to tell herself, "One man has rejected me. That's his loss. I can find love again."

Burns believes that as we become aware that our thoughts precede—and determine—our feelings, and as we learn to control our thoughts, we can banish depression. This is happy news for those of us who battle more than a few blue hours or days. This approach gives us the feeling we are not pawns in the universe or helpless victims because of our early lives. Rather, we are people who can actively help ourselves.

And if we don't exert our wills? Then we can be lured into deeper darkness.

Perhaps no celebrated life illustrates the volitional aspect of depression better than that of poet and mother, Sylvia Plath. Plath committed suicide when she was thirty, just after the publication of her novel *Bell Jar* and shortly after separating from her husband, poet Ted Hughes, who was involved in an affair. In her biography of Plath called *Bitter Fame*, Anne Stevenson chronicles Plath's deliberate descent into darkness.[13]Plath, who had attempted suicide at age twenty, lost her father to death when she was eleven. She wrote obsessively about death and was filled with rage at her father and God. *Ariel*, her last collection of poems, is the work of a gifted depressive who courted the guardians of the dark gates.

Scrambling to Safety

It was liberating when I finally discovered I did not have to give in to my tendency toward depression, making myself and others miserable. I was not chemically depressed; I had just learned to think negatively about myself and my future. Therefore, I could *choose* to help myself. I could *choose* to seek the company of others when I felt, as a writer, too isolated. I could also redefine myself and let go of the perfectionism that has dogged my steps. In addition, I could begin to deal with all those early losses. It is overly simplistic to say we choose to be depressed. We can, however, choose to get the help we need.

Karen admits that at one level she wanted to remain depressed. "I deliberately gave in to it," she says. "It was as if I deserved to be depressed. I know that sounds schizophrenic—to cry out to God while sinking into despair, though I didn't see it at the time. But I can remember both kinds of thoughts."

We remain in the darkness at our own peril. If we allow the darkness to engulf us, we may not be able to combat the inertia that sets in. We must learn to catch ourselves at the beginning of our downhill slide. As we monitor our self-talk, we fight back. We can substitute rational, positive thoughts for negative ones. Also, we can engage in some self-care and nurture the woman inside.

Programming Pleasure into Our Lives

The woman who is depressed usually deprives herself of pleasurable activities. Feeling worthless, she becomes increasingly paralyzed. David Burns says that depressives suffer from "do nothingism." His answer is to have clients log daily activities, as well as to make lists of activities that yield fun and pleasure. He believes people feel better when they become productive and engage in activities that nourish the spirit.

I enjoy lunches out with other women. This is somewhere

near the top of my "pleasurable activities list" (after quality time with my husband and daughters). When I feel, because of school or writing, that my solitude is leaving me prey to low feelings, I schedule time with good friends. I immediately feel better even after scheduling the luncheon date on the phone!

What activities do you enjoy? If it's tennis, schedule a match next week. The physical activity as well as the social time will serve as a tonic. If you like to shop, golf, or drive in the country, call another mother, pack a picnic lunch, and pile the kids in the car for an excursion.

Maybe you enjoy art galleries or museums or reading poetry. If so, find the time, even a few hours a week. Sometimes what a woman needs is a "room of one's own," a place to retreat to pursue activities that nourish the spirit and define the self. Said one young mother, "I'm going to engage a sitter a few hours each week so I can retreat to a room upstairs to read, write, and think my own thoughts."

Friendship is also a buffer against depression. Yet I have been surprised at how few women seek emotional support from their friends.

Once after I had spoken about depression to a group of young mothers, I asked how many saw a friend once a week. Out of twenty women, only one raised her hand. Several indicated they took the kids to McDonald's once a month with another mother. "I am lucky if I have a heart-to-heart talk with a good friend every six months," said a woman who had talked about her own private struggle with depression. As I left the group that day, I realized how poor some of us are at providing self-care. We fail to seek the companionship that will not only keep us from getting depressed, but makes life more enjoyable as well.

Mothers' Support Groups

Several years ago three other mothers and I formed Home by Choice, a national organization to encourage mothers at home. One of the things we four believed strongly was that mothers at home need help in creating supportive networks. We concluded that a major thrust of Home by Choice would be to help mothers start and run support groups that would meet either weekly or biweekly to discuss topics of interest.

The focus of the HBC mothers' support groups, then, is to provide parenting information and education, as well as encouragement and emotional support. We hope that friendships will develop and that women will flourish as a result of finding other mothers who share their Judeo-Christian values.

Psychological research confirms that we women need emotional support throughout our lives, but especially when we have young children. Bowlby has said that mothers of young children are vulnerable and need all the help and support they can get.[14] The nuclear family is in dire straits and many parents feel powerless. A way to combat this feeling of powerlessness (and the absence of extended family) is to encourage women to create meaningful networks.

Home by Choice is only one of many support groups springing up around the country, indicating that mothers at home are hungry for some recognition of their needs. A number have told me that after only a brief period in an HBC support group, they feel much better about themselves as mothers and about their decision to stay home. Listen to one woman describe her experience.

Cheryl Crigger Morgan, a CPA, experienced culture shock when she and her husband moved to Washington,

D. C., from her hometown in Charleston, West Virginia. Knowing no one, Cheryl and her three-year-old daughter spent a number of days alone after the move until a neighbor invited her to an HBC support group.

Cheryl, who was four-and-a-half-months pregnant, was pleased to meet another mother whose due date was close to her own. "I was so excited to finally be with other women my age and have adult conversations that I spoke as rapidly as was humanly possible," says Cheryl. "Fortunately, no one seemed to notice."

According to Cheryl, the HBC support group helped make her transition easier. Having worked "crazy hours" as a CPA during most of her daughter's life, Cheryl was unprepared for the unstructured life at home. With the group's help, however, she was "able to feel good about leaving the work force and approach life at home with greater confidence." Most important, Cheryl found close friendships within the group—women who celebrated the birth of her son, Grant, with her and her husband.

Had she remained alone at home, Cheryl might have become depressed. Instead, she found invaluable support and friendship. As a result, her self-esteem soared, and she has made the transition from the office to home in fine style.

Belonging to a support group where a mother can share her feelings honestly is a powerful boost for flagging self-esteem. One woman said, "I haven't thought about low self-esteem for about a year—the same period of time I've been in this group. I guess being with other moms who share my values has made me feelstronger."

We women crave emotional support, and to stay out of the depression pit we need to nurture ourselves through friendship with other women as well as plan activities that provide pleasure and meaning in our lives.

For many women, this will be enough. They received sufficient parental love growing up that they struggle with only occasional blue hours or days. But what about the woman who suffers from heavy-duty depression—that woman I call *the unnurtured self?* How can she find the love and healing she so desperately yearns for? Where does she go for relief from pain? And who can possibly understand her deepest hurts?

Healing the Wounded Self

Success is counted sweetest
By those who ne'er succeed,
To comprehend a nectar
Requires the sorest need—
                    Emily Dickinson

Sophie sat on our chintz sofa, stroking our overweight calico cat, Muhammad, who reclined in her lap. Sophie, an emigré who left Moscow six years ago, began to tell her story in halting English.

"My mother went to work part-time when I was a little girl, and then when I was four, my parents divorced and my mother started to work full-time. I was sent to a neighbor who lived nearby, but her children resented me. They said, 'Why don't you go to your own home?' and I would cry. Then when my mother came home at night, I was difficult and she punished me."

Sophie hit her chest with her fist. "I have always felt something was missing," she said. "Something here," and she hit her chest again.

I sat quietly, resisting the impulse to put my arms around this woman who looked so much like a distressed child. I sensed what Sophie needed was to "own" her pain and feel my comforting presence across the room. She continued, voicing an old, deep woe that seemed to emerge from her most primitive self. Sophie said she had longed for her father's love, but because her mother had been so embittered, she refused to allow Sophie to even see him. Sophie cried quietly, her shoulders heaving.

Struggling to regain her composure, Sophie said, "Now when I try to play with my child—she's two—I can't. I want to, I really do, but somehow I just can't."

"I understand," I responded, knowing that this woman who had failed to experience sensitive, caring mothering would have had a hard time giving to her child. As one child psychologist said, "To do good mothering, you have to receive it." Sophie's mother had not been present, either physically or emotionally, for her daughter in early childhood. Moreover, she had been insensitive to Sophie's losses, so it was understandable that Sophie was having great difficulty responding to her small daughter.

In truth, Sophie needed to be mothered herself. Only as she finds nurture for her unnurtured self can she break out of those patterns of attachment—the insecurity—her mother and father bequeathed to her. This chapter, then, is for those mothers who wish to be home to their children but, because of their attachment histories, feel they are inadequate mothers.

Our Mothers/Our Selves

In 1977 Nancy Friday published *My Mother/Myself*, which became a national bestseller. In her book Friday explored the complex relationship a daughter has with her mother.

Speaking for herself and for other women, Friday wrote: "All my life I had shown the world an independent person, a brave exterior that hid the frightened child within. This split in which I had lived had sapped my strength, leaving me divided against myself. The split had begun to heal when my writing forced me to recognize that my fears and angers were those a child felt toward a mother of long ago who was also a woman, like myself."[1]

Friday wrote about the conflictual and distant relationship she had with her mother. Her story helped other women to recognize their mothers were key players in their adult lives, influencing their capacity to parent and their feelings about themselves as women.

In keeping with Bowlby's attachment theory, psychologist Seymour Epstein believes a woman's level of self-esteem in adulthood is highly correlated with her mother's acceptance or rejection of her in childhood.[2] Those women who experienced responsive mothering in childhood tend to have high self-esteem in adulthood; those women whose mothers were insensitive or rejecting in childhood, struggle with low self-esteem and feelings of depression. To feel "love worthiness" as an adult, a woman needs her mother's accepting love early in her life.

This high self-esteem enables us to parent well. A study of twenty-eight mothers with their infants supports this theory. The researchers studied children who were one year old and found that those mothers who had securely attached children not only reported higher self-esteem, but also had positive memories of childhood relationships with their mothers, fathers, and peers. The women who had anxiously-attached children reported less acceptance from their parents than did the mothers of the securely attached children.[3]

Another study found that the mothers of infants who avoided them in the reunion episodes of the Strange Situation (see chapter 3) had memories of unresolved maternal rejection in childhood. However, if the mothers in this study were in touch with their feelings of rejection and felt anger towards their mothers, their babies were securely attached.[4]

Implications of the Research

What are the implications of this research? Attachment patterns get passed on cross-generationally. A daughter who has experienced maternal rejection may have difficulty creating a secure attachment relationship with her own child. Notice, however, that those mothers who were in touch with their feelings, who had "worked through" maternal rejection, had securely attached children. The key, then, is to understand or "own" the past and "work it through" to some new place of forgiveness and healing.

I have spoken with enough women, however, to know that some find this extremely hard to do. Either they have denied painful memories or they feel that to examine the parental relationship is tantamount to betrayal.

Recently, I met a young mother who said she had almost no memories of her dead mother. "This is curious," she continued, "because I was nearly thirteen when my mother died." A few moments later she acknowledged she had never felt close to her mother—a tipoff that she was blocking painful memories. This woman also indicated she was having difficulty relating to her own adolescent daughter, and this was generating pain for her.

I suggested that because she desired to be close to her own child, she had a wonderful opportunity to look at her past, particularly the relationship with her mother, to examine the lack of closeness and all she had missed. "I know it will hurt," she said reflectively. "Yes," I said, "but you are carrying pain now, and it's far better to look at it and get rid of it."

But how does a mother become aware of her unnurtured past with its ramifications? There are many ways "home."

In *The Art of Psychotherapy* Anthony Storr writes: "In psychotherapy, many of the things which the patient discovers about himself are things which he may say that he has known all along but has never clearly recognized. . . . Putting things into words, like writing an examination paper, clarifies both what one knows or what one does not know."[5] Storr indicates that as one verbalizes painful material, he can then begin to critically evaluate his emotions.

In addition, a therapist can trace connections between events, symptoms, and personality characteristics which are not immediately obvious. As the therapist does this, he is, in effect, attempting to change a person's internal working models. "Psychotherapy then becomes what has been called a 'corrective emotional experience,' " says Storr, "in which negative assumptions about other people are gradually modified by means of the repeated analysis of the patient's changing relationship with the therapist."[6] Basically, the therapist "re-parents" the patient through the process of transference. By finding someone who values and understands him, the patient is then able to "generalize" that he will get better treatment from others than he initially received from his parents.[7]

Simply put, this means that as a wounded mother "owns" her pain, examines past events, better understands her own mother, and forgives, she can experience greater intimacy with others and be a better parent to her children.

"Mothering Mom"

There are, however, other paths to inner healing than traditional psychotherapy.

One well-respected intervention model was created by Selma Fraiberg to help hurting, deprived mothers whose infants were failing to thrive. In the Fraiberg Intervention Model, a trained therapist visits the mother in her own home. Initially the visits focus on the needs of the baby who is not developing as he should. Later as the therapist focuses on the mother's needs as well as the baby's, the mother is often able to talk about her own impoverished life. As she grieves over the inadequate mothering she received, she begins the process toward healing and becoming a better mother.[8]

Fraiberg writes of a little boy named Billy who was referred to the Infant Mental Health Program at the University of Michigan because he was starving. Five months old, Billy vomited every time he was fed and had gained no weight over a three month period. Although he weighed eight pounds at birth, Billy weighed only fourteen pounds at five months; he was a "tense, morose, somber baby who looked 'like a little old man.' "[9]

The therapist visited the home and watched as Kathie, Billy's seventeen-year-old mother, placed the baby and bottle on the floor. Billy crept toward his bottle, grasping it hungrily, and Kathie said, "He likes it that way. He likes to have his bottle alone, on the floor."[10] Not only did Kathie withhold nourishment from Billy, but she also held him face down over the bathroom sink after he had taken his bottle to ensure that he would not vomit on her. Thus, Kathie was preventing her baby from gaining any weight and guaranteeing that he was always hungry.

The therapist understood that by nurturing Kathie, she would eventually enable Kathie to become a better mother. But at first the therapist concentrated on showing Kathie how to feed and burp Billy. Then she helped apathetic little Billy establish eye contact with his mother, since Billy often looked away from Kathie.

To bring this about, the therapist ingeniously asked Kathie if she ever told Billy any stories. When she said no, the therapist proceeded to tell both mother and child the story of the three bears, using voice inflections. Writes Fraiberg: "Billy and his mother *both* loved the story. Billy began to smile and make eye contact with the therapist and his mother, as together they watched him. Kathie so enjoyed this herself, as both child and mother, that she herself began to tell Billy stories and, of course, Billy quickly began to respond."[11]

In time the therapist encouraged Kathie to talk about her painful past. Kathie spoke "with great sadness" about her relationship with her mother. Apparently, she could never please her mother, who overtly rejected her. As she talked, Kathie cried and scolded the mother "who never heard her cries and needs."[12] During subsequent visits, as Kathie worked through her pain and voiced her unmet needs, she became more empathic and comforting toward her son. "When Kathie's own cries were heard by the therapist," writes Fraiberg, "she began to respond to her baby's cries."[13]

Kathie's story is a powerful example of the hope that exists for any mother who failed to experience sufficient mothering in her own childhood. If an unnurtured mother can find a caring, empathic individual to nurture her, she may find balm for her wounded soul.

But must this nurturer always be a trained clinician? That depends on how wounded the mother is.

A mother who is dealing with great inner devastation will most likely need to work with a trained professional. But I am impressed that we humans are programmed toward mental health, and we will seek help and utilize it whenever we can find it. Surcease from pain and greater psychological growth may come from relationships with others, particularly older women who are caring, empathic people. If a caring person can become "a secure base," someone to be counted on and trusted, then she can become a nurturer and, ultimately, a healer for a hurting younger mother.

Home Start, a London-based program launched more than ten years ago, utilizes "ordinary" mothers in the healing process. Isolated mothers who are at risk for child abuse are provided the opportunity for weekly visits, not from a mental health professional, but from the mother of a school-age child.[14] Bowlby called this "mothering mom," indicating that the more support a hurting mom has, the better off she will be. He noted that in all the years the program has been operational, not one mother has gone on to physically abuse her baby. Instead, many have themselves become volunteers in the program.

Harvard's Karlen Lyons-Ruth and her colleagues investigated the effects of weekly home visits on a disadvantaged population. In this study of depressed mothers whose infants who were at risk for lower mental and language development, mothers and babies were visited weekly in their homes by ordinary mothers, as well as by psychologists. The researchers found that the home-visited infants were further along in their development than the infants who were not visited.[15] Also the home-visited infants were *twice* as likely to be securely attached to their mothers.

The researchers focused on the mother's need for positive emotional support. They modeled different behavior with her baby, teaching the mother certain actions they wished her to emulate. Also, they were extremely supportive of the mother-child relationship, and in keeping with the Fraiberg model, attempted to build the mother's self-esteem.

At an infant attachment conference I attended recently, the consensus of the experts was that mothers of infants are extremely responsive to intervention. Moreover, these experts said it's not that difficult to put a mother "back on the parenting track" if her deep needs begin to be met and she receives parenting education and "well-informed" outside help in parenting her child.

So intervention is another method for helping the unnurtured mother and tutoring her in more effective parenting. But professionals are not the only ones who can give this kind of help. London's Home Start program and Lyons-Ruth's research both indicate that other, more experienced mothers can nurture unnurtured moms as well.

A Personal Aside

Several years ago I sat where Sophie sat, on the same chintz sofa, aware like her that something vital was missing. All the old issues I thought I had resolved years earlier came back to haunt me, and I was confused. Why? I wondered. Why was I troubled by things I had worked through earlier in my thirties?

At age forty-two I found myself confronting the painful issue of loss. This was triggered, in part, by the fact that Holly and Kristen were readying to leave home for college, and they were in the throes of what psychologists call the separation-individuation process. My relationship with my daughters had meant the world to me, and it hurt terribly to think they would soon leave my home. At bottom, I feared they would leave my life.

I did not know then what I have since learned—that if we release our children, they will come back as friends. All I felt during that time was fear and loss. As my dependency needs heightened, I even became afraid of losing Don's love. After all, I reasoned, Thomas had left years earlier. Would everyone go? As a result of my inner turmoil, Don and I went through a period of marital tension and strife as I clung to him. It didn't help that I was also caught in the throes of hormonal changes due to menopause.

I needed to talk to someone about my inner turmoil. The unhealed places were simply too pervasive to ignore. Feeling estranged from my husband, my children, myself, I finally went into therapy with a clinical psychologist who zeroed in on my relationship with my mother. Relentlessly, he hammered away at my defenses: my fear of betraying my mother, all my excuses for her behavior, my eternal hope that someday she would recover from the emotional illness that worsened during my adolescence and finally meet my emotional needs. Once Dr. Raban even shouted at me, "Give her up. Let her go." As a popular song says, I had a "fortress around my heart."

During this period, I prayed that God would heal me and help me let go of my mother. I could not handle the turmoil any longer. Psychiatry and psychology, as I understood them, were effective at diagnosing human ills, but could psychotherapy exorcise the soul? My psychologist had said that the best psychotherapy can do is help people control symptoms. "Therapy does not heal the soul," he said. Anthony Storr says that the psychotherapeutic cure "means to be able to modify and make use of one's psychopathology rather than getting rid of it."[16]

Yet I longed for more than symptom control or harnessing my psychopathology. I wanted to be free from psychological pain and live a happier, freer life. Thus, I prayed, "God, I don't understand this mother yearning or how to get rid of it, but I'm asking you to take it away." And then I tried some honest manipulation. I added: "If you don't heal me, how can I ever tell anyone that you set us free?"

As I continued to work through painful issues in therapy and simultaneously asked God to make me more whole, a wonderful thing happened. One day I noticed that the old yearning had simply disappeared. Inside, all was quiet. Unlike the maternally deprived writer Richard Rhodes, I no longer had "a hole in [my] world."

Not surprisingly, my marriage improved and my relationship with my daughters changed for the better. Although I had been close to them, I could finally let them go. They, who had meant so much to their "affect hungry" mother, could finally leave home physically and psychologically. Moreover, I was soon able to change my relationship with my own mother.

Within a year my mother arrived unexpectedly for two weeks, and for the first time in my adult life, I felt peace in her presence. I was finally able to accept her as she is—not as I wished she would be. I realized my mother could give physical, though not emotional, nurture. An industrious woman, she washed dishes after every meal, helped me with organizational correspondence, and ironed the mountain of clothes that permanently resides in the ironing basket. During her stay we avoided all those topics she finds hard to handle, and not a sharp word was spoken. When mother finally left, I walked into the room where she stayed and cried. Those two weeks of calm between us had been a great gift.

I had finally made peace with my only living parent.

I had finally made peace with myself.

Another way we find healing is through the love of our children. As we care for them from infancy on, we are constantly challenged to seek greater wholeness—for their sakes. They love us without reserve, believing we are gods and goddesses in the early years.

I shall always be grateful that I have been a mother. As my daughters have trusted me since infancy, their love has remade me. Because I wanted greater wholeness for them than I ever experienced, I have struggled to grow to meet the challenges that good parenting requires. Oh, I've blown it many, many times, but today we are emotionally close and have honest communication. My children have been one of my life's greatest gifts.

From my own experience, I know that with the help of a compassionate therapist, one can travel down the road toward inner healing. Yet sometimes therapy alone isn't enough. Research shows that only about half of those who go into traditional psychotherapy find relief from their symptoms. When one is in pain, one wants better odds for recovery. Sometimes God has to settle our subterranean wars and set us free from the destructive patterns of the past—our cross-generational legacy.

A man who experienced this phenomenon is Roger Helle, a former Vietnam veteran. When Roger and his twin brother were four, their father, an abusive man, abandoned the family, and the brothers were placed in an orphanage. Helle's mother, an alcoholic, remarried years later and came to get her sons. But Helle found no relief for a pervasive sense of loneliness and worthlessness in his new home with a workaholic stepfather. Leaving home at eighteen, Helle enlisted in the Marines and headed for Vietnam. Caring little about himself, Helle says he "volunteered for every dangerous mission I could."[17] Later wounded by an exploding grenade, Helle lay dying in a hospital in Da Nang. As he lay there, unable to speak, Helle cried out in his spirit, "God, let me live and I'll do anything you want."[18]

Helle lived, returned to the States, married, and forgot his promise. Only when he was unable to create marital intimacy and divorce was imminent did he remember that earlier event—the time God had been close and had restored his physical health. Asking God to save his marriage, Helle seemingly became aware for the first time that he had worth, not with his parents but with God.

That awareness produced personality change, and Helle and his wife enjoyed a richer, more intimate marriage. Today both are involved through Teen Challenge in helping young people who, because of feelings of worthlessness, are drug users. Now himself the father of a son, Helle says he looks at his son and says, "I love you, Joshua. I can't tell you how much you're worth."[19]

In sum, though we bring our early experience into our later relationships—and change is difficult—it is *not* inevitable that we remain captive to our past. Nor is it inevitable that we pass on cross-generational patterns of attachment. Neglect, rejection, and abuse do not *invariably* breed the same conditions in subsequent generations. What is important is that people have "corrective emotional experiences" that change their internal working models.[20] That is, we need to have intense, emotional experiences that change our long-held concepts of ourselves and others. Personality change is difficult but it is possible, particularly when old issues demand resolution.

It happened to me. Home became a place of healing once I stopped running, owned the pain, and confronted the past with all its wrack and ruin. Home can be a place of healing for you, too, when the "former desolations" of the spirit are repaired.

But what about our husbands? Sometimes it is the husband who has a broken, deprived past. How does a woman best understand and nurture the man in her life?

The Man in Her Life

Our early lessons in love and our
developmental history shape the
expectations we bring into marriage.
Judith Viorst

Once a woman becomes a mother, the man in her life
assumes ever greater importance; no longer just husband,
lover, friend, the man she loves is now also the father of
her child. Not only is he a more powerful figure, but the
marital stakes are higher: she wonders how her husband
will respond to her greater dependency and vulnerability
now that she has a baby to care for. Does he possess the
emotional and psychological resources to become a good
father? Will he support her compelling need to be a good
mother?

The pressures in any marriage increase after the birth
of the first child. No longer two relatively independent
beings sharing a marital dream, now a man and woman
must interface on a hundred fronts as they share a parenting dream. And the most significant blueprint each brings

to the task of parenting is the one acquired during the earliest years.

In her book *Necessary Losses*, poet Judith Viorst writes that we "bring into marriage the unconscious longings and the unfinished business of childhood, and prompted by the past, we make demands in our marriage, unaware that we do."[1]

Viorst says the marital state is characterized by both love and hate. In marriage, men and women attempt to reclaim (or discover for the first time) mother's unconditional love; if they fail, they "hate" the mate for withholding what is needed. "We do not, of course, enter marriage with the conscious intention of marrying daddy—or mommy," says Viorst. "Our hidden agenda is also hidden from us."[2] She adds, "But subterranean hopes make for seismic disturbances."[3]

As noted earlier in the discussion of my own research, the birth of a child is a time when a woman may rethink her own parenting history. It is also a time when she needs for her husband to be especially sensitive to her needs for emotional support as she is giving to her newborn around the clock. And its a time when she needs to understand him and what drives him and his fathering.

The Wife's Needs

I had a conversation recently with Beverly, a young mother who carried a carrot-haired seven-month-old daughter. "What do I do," she asked, "when my husband urges me to go back to work?"

"That's tough," I replied. "Did he have a full-time working mother?" When she slowly nodded her head yes, I added, "That means he doesn't see any need for you to be home with your baby, right?"

Seeing the connection, Beverly responded quickly, "That's true. My husband tells me he was raised by nannies and he turned out all right, so why shouldn't his child also be raised by a babysitter?"

This young mother had raised a thorny issue I frequently encounter. From conversations with women over the years, I know that Beverly is not alone. Numerous women have told me they want to stay home, but their husbands demand that they work. Some say their husbands are afraid to be the sole provider and depend psychologically on that second income; others indicate that their husbands like to brag about the wife's job and fear marriage to a housewife. One justice department lawyer said, "My mother never worked. We have nothing to talk about any more. That's why I want my wife to have a career."

But what if a woman's heart tells her that her children need her at home at the same time her husband pushes her to get a job? She will obviously experience great turmoil. She is hurt if her husband fails to understand her need to nurture her baby or their baby's need for exclusive maternal care.

If a husband makes such a demand, I believe he is probably unwittingly recreating his own emotional pain.

Let me explain. If a man had a mother who was physically or emotionally absent for most of his childhood—if he was raised by babysitters or a succession of other caretakers—he will most likely not know what emotional closeness or intimacy feels like. So how can he possibly know what his child is missing? Also, he probably won't be in touch with his feelings. Perhaps in childhood, he simply walled off his anger and his yearning for closeness by repressing these unfulfilled emotions.

If I were to describe such a man, I would say he is efficient, aloof, possibly a workaholic. His wife might describe him as cold and distant. She probably longs to be close to him but finds it hard, so she is excited about the possibility of establishing intimate connections with her new baby. The husband may even unconsciously feel jealous of the duo without fully understanding why.

Rob is an engineer who urged his wife Annelise to return to her job as a pediatric nurse shortly after the birth of their first child, David. Rob's mother worked with his father in their country store in Louisiana. Although both parents were nearby—the store was next to Rob's house—they worked long hours, and Rob's mother was preoccupied with housework when she wasn't doing the bookkeeping. Rob remembers lonely, solitary days as an only child.

He says with pride that he became emotionally independent at an early age. Unable to show his feelings, Rob doesn't understand that his infant son needs something a babysitter can't supply. Besides, he and Annelise use the money she earns for vacations, dinners out, new clothes. A pediatric nurse who was close to her own mother, Annelise knows her baby needs her. Moreover, she is afraid David will become too attached to the sitter. She's frustrated, she can't change Rob's mind, and her emotional pain is becoming more intense as time passes. The couple fights, but they can't seem to resolve their dilemma.

But it's not only the husband who urges his wife to return to work who creates conflict. So too does the husband who reluctantly agrees to have his wife stay home. This man is also insensitive to his wife's need to nurture and be nurtured in return. Said a friend, "How can any woman feel good about what she's doing if her husband only *grudgingly* allows her to stay home with the kids?"

Ford, Meridith's husband, falls into this category. He is openly critical of the way his wife manages their home and cares for their children. "Meridith used to manage major accounts as a stockbroker," says Ford, "but now she is overwhelmed by a toddler and a baby. I came home the other day and our son was in the living room playing with plastic bags! What could she have been thinking of?" Ford adds that he occasionally keeps the kids, and has found that it's no big thing.

Caring for small children is a difficult task. They make unremitting demands, or so it seems at times. A mother can feel overwhelmed if she is caring for a toddler and an infant simultaneously. When my own daughters were very young, I felt like a "giving machine." I even made up a little rhyme that I chanted when they clamored:

> One mother, two hands,
> Two children, making demands.

How many men are willing to handle what a mother of small children deals with regularly? Said one male psychologist, "You don't see men rushing home to change diapers and feed their babies." True. But whether he spends hours caretaking or not, every father has a vital role in providing emotional support for his wife. For a mother to do effective mothering she needs not only a harmonious marriage, but she also needs for her husband to be emotionally supportive. Any woman who lives in a chaotic marriage without sufficient emotional support cannot possibly devote herself fully to mothering. Her baby's clamorous needs will be more than she can effectively cope with. So a husband needs to understand his strategic role in fostering his wife's sense of well-being.

Understanding Post-Feminist Males

But just as a woman needs to be supported in her mothering, so too does a man need his fair share of understanding and support in marriage. According to writer Sam Allis, post-feminist males are "confused, angry and desperately seeking manhood."[4] Allis adds that men are speaking up in locker rooms across America about their rancor at being criticized for their inadequacies in boardroom and bedroom. "They are airing their frustration," says Allis, "with the limited roles they face today, compared with the multiple options that women seem to have won."

American males are not only angry and confused, Allis says, but they are exhausted from trying to live up to performance standards they feel women impose. Modern men must be sensitive, but not wimps; they should exhibit "tempered macho," and be super successful in their careers.

It's tough, says Allis, to be a man today. Modern man faces not only the difficult challenge of forming a sense of identity in liberationist America, but he is also unlikely to find much love and acceptance from a woman in the process.

Father Daniel O'Connell, a Jesuit priest and psychologist on the faculty of Georgetown University, further explains the male quandary: "I am convinced that when a woman becomes an abrasive feminist, she competes with a man on his own turf. She encourages the very chauvinism she objects to because she is being chauvinistic herself. This makes it impossible for a man to show gentleness and reverence for women."

Father O'Connell believes men today are needy. "They need to be instructed and informed," he says, "in an atmosphere that isn't threatening. That is precisely what the gentle woman provides. A gentle woman can teach a man to be gentle, respectful, and reverent of her womanhood as complementary to his own manhood."

Some psychologists would have us believe males are more physically and psychologically vulnerable than females. Psychologist Dee Shepherd-Look (1982) writes that from conception, males are more susceptible than females to every type of "physical disease, developmental difficulty and environmental assault."[5] Although 140 males are conceived for every 100 females, 35 of these male fetuses will die during gestation. Three-fourths of all babies stillborn before four months are males.

Additionally, males are more vulnerable to malnutrition, and they are more likely than females to have speech, learning, and behavior problems. They are also three to five times more likely to have reading problems. In the arena of emotional disorders, more males than females suffer from night terrors, hyperactivity, and autism.

Moreover, adolescent males have a higher incidence of schizophrenia, delinquency, academic underachievement, and suicide than females. Writes Shepherd-Look, "Until adulthood, it is difficult to find a pathological condition in which the incidence among females is higher than among males."[6]

Boys are also more likely to suffer if mom returns to the work force than are girls. Researcher Michael Lamb says that in studies of elementary school children, sons appear to suffer when mother works outside the home.[7] Effects, however, differ in lower-class and middle-class families. In lower-class families, sons have difficulty with their fathers when the mother works. Lamb believes that in these families maternal employment represents the father's failure to provide for the family, and this creates tension. In middle-class families, sons of employed mothers do not do as well academically as sons of mothers at home.

The point of this brief examination of male vulnerability is to assert that sons and husbands need the women in their lives to nurture them, appreciate them, and express interest in their lives. As little boys or as high-powered executives, males suffer from female neglect.

Ralph, a corporate manager, believes that all men need sensitive women in their lives. "A sensitive woman," says Ralph, "can get quickly to the heart of the matter. We men dance around personal issues. We're competitive and don't probe the way women do." We women are able to do this because all our lives we have focused on relationships and our human connections. Men speak the language of the rational mind with an emphasis on separateness whereas we speak from the heart, our perceptions grounded in connectedness.

While men and women speak different languages, each sex assumes they speak the same.[8]

Shortly after they were married, Bruce and Marissa discovered he spoke "Swahili" and she spoke "Urdu." Marissa didn't really understand Bruce in the heat of an argument, and while he said he understood her, she knew he didn't. It was only after seeing the movie *Beaches* that Bruce emerged from the darkened theater enlightened. Having watched the two female protagonists communicate with considerable heat, Bruce said, "There's no way a man can speak on such a wide range of personal subjects with that kind of emotional intensity."

Nurturing Our Husbands

So how do we nurture our husbands? First, we need to look beneath the exterior and see the man inside. It is easy to feel that a 6'2" man with a chest size of 42" is invulnerable. Though men possess greater physical strength than women, they are easily hurt. This may be difficult to grasp, particularly if a woman had a distant relationship with a detached father or no relationship at all.

Because I grew up without a father or a brother, I have had difficulty understanding what men are like. As I've mentioned, I did feel close to my grandfather, but I didn't live long with him on a daily basis. So when I approached adult men in my twenties, they were something of a mystery to me. My husband Don has worked hard to demythologize the mythic male by showing me his soft, vulnerable side. Remember, he says, that inside every man still lurks a little boy. Recently, I became freshly acquainted with this little boy in my husband on a trip to Iowa for his college reunion.

As we stood in front of the unpretentious white frame house still standing on Main Street in Hamilton, Illinois, Don told me about the happiness he had experienced there during the first seven years of his life. "This is the ditch where I fell and cut my knee," said Don, standing near a culvert in front of the white house. "The cut was deep enough that my knee required a splint. My friends then pulled me around town in a red wagon for three days." His tone of voice had just a touch of pride. Under the spell of his memories, my husband's face changed, softened, and years fell away. With obvious emotion, Don spoke of one adventure after another that transpired in his safe, contained world of childhood. And I understood, as never before, the meaning these early friendships had in my husband's life.

After his early years, Don's parents moved frequently, and Don found it harder to make and keep friends. He had friends, he told me, but the relationships weren't as deep or as meaningful as his earliest carefree friendships in small town Hamilton. Don's high school experience in Chicago was particularly lonely since he had to take a streetcar to school and his buddies lived in another neighborhood across town. The situation was exacerbated because Don's parents were not especially interested in having his friends visit their home.

On that trip I understood more clearly why my husband loved his small college in Dubuque, Iowa. There, just as in Hamilton, he was encircled by friends. There he found soulmates. As student body president, he was king of the road again, just as he had been, cruising the sidewalks in his little red wagon.

When we attended his class reunion, his fellow alumni responded to Don as they remembered him thirty-five years ago, and I saw my husband in a new way. Before my eyes, this gray-haired lawyer became, once again, fraternity brother, friend, "prez."

I realized anew that it strengthens a marriage and is nurturing to a man for a wife to try to understand who he was in his early relationships and how he has changed over time. To peer inside at the child our husbands once were, with all their fears, longings, and rich experiences, is to get in touch with their soft side. This was brought home to me at Don's reunion when I spoke to a professor's wife about her sons. When I asked if she missed having daughters, she replied, "Oh, no. My boys, who are eight and ten, love to play sports and go hunting with their father, but they also enjoy talking to me about their feelings."

We gain a more complete understanding of that man who walks tall and exudes competence at work and at home if we understand this. My husband is an optimistic, competent man who by his own admission awakens every morning with high energy and a cheerful outlook on life. But the longer we live together the more facets I see of this man who shares his hurts, longings, hopes, and desires. And after seventeen years, it seems we have only just begun.

Father Hunger

In understanding our husbands, we also need to examine along with them their early relationships with their parents, particularly their fathers. I have talked to a number of men who suffer from "father hunger." This is the term coined by James Herzog, assistant professor of psychiatry at Harvard, to describe young children who experienced prolonged separations from their fathers.[9] In my experience, many men suffer from father hunger, not only from fathers who were absent, but also from fathers who were passive or uninvolved.

Gene, a thirty-two year old physician, is the son of an IBM manager in his sixties. His dad, a silent, religious man, was home most evenings and weekends. An active member of his church, this man dutifully paid his bills, cared for his wife and their sons, but seldom connected with his sons emotionally. "I don't remember that he ever hugged me or played ball with me," says Gene reflectively. "He absolutely never told me about his feelings. I have distinct memories of my father standing alone, staring out the window. At times, he seemed like a ghost to me."

Rich, at fifty-five, had a similar experience with his father, a now-retired business man. His father never told him that he loved him. "We just started to shake hands a few years ago," says Rich. "The stress of managing a small

town newspaper engulfed him. You heard about other
people taking family vacations, but we never did. We never
sat down to talk." Rich does remember that once in high
school he asked his dad to advise him about a problem.
"Only that once did we drop our guard," says Rich. Rich
says he believes his father is committed to him and loves
him, but his dad simply cannot express his feelings. A man
who still longs for his father's touch, Rich says that for him
to hug his dad now would be like "diving off a high diving
board."

Our Husbands/Their Fathers

Writer Michel Marriott addresses this same issue in his
article, "Father Hunger."[10] Fathered by a harsh and unaf-
fectionate man, Michel says he cannot relate intimately
with his father and struggles to do so with his son. He fears
that his relationship with his son just may not "hold."[11]

Former professional football player Bill Glass, who
works with prisoners, says if a man is denied his father's
affirmation or blessing, he will search for it all his life.[12]
The absence of a father's acceptance and unconditional
love can, according to Glass, cause a man to become an
overachiever or a convict. "I have never met an inmate
who loves his dad," says Glass, who has worked in six hundred prisons over the last twenty years. "They'll make
excuses for their moms, but they hate their dads' guts.
There's something that makes a man mean when he
doesn't get along with his father. It makes him dangerous.
You better not turn your back on him."

Glass feels strongly that all fathers need to confer a
blessing (approval) on their children, but especially their
sons, through touch and verbal affirmation. He has no
patience with fathers who simply expect their children to

know intuitively that they love them. "A blessing is not a blessing until you say it," says Glass, who regularly tells his sons that he loves them and that they are "fantastic." Glass's sons are both 6'6" and weigh in at 285 and 275 pounds. Recently, Glass grabbed his elder son and said he loved him. "Tears welled up in his eyes," says Glass. "They always do." Glass believes that we never outgrow our need for our father's blessing.

Finally, Glass believes that not only should fathers touch and verbally affirm their sons, but they must never withdraw their unconditional love. He notes that when parents of runaway kids are contacted, two out of three say they don't want their children to come home. That is hardly unconditional, committed love.

Glass believes children need, ultimately, to be affirmed by both parents, though he admits most people he's encountered have never experienced this.

So what can you do if you have been denied the parental blessing? Glass suggests if a parent is alive that you should go to him and ask for it. And if the parent is dead? "Then go to the grave and forgive him," says Glass, "otherwise you'll become bitter." On a more positive note, Glass says you should consider finding a father substitute who will confer the blessing.

But what is a woman to do who finds herself and her children affected by her husband's father hunger? Struggling with his own low self-esteem, her husband will not know how to get close to his wife and children.

Melanie and John: A Marriage that Changed

John grew up in a middle-class family in the south with a father who indicated repeatedly that his son, an underachiever and poor athlete, failed to measure up to his expectations. A busy bank executive, John's father also served on the local school board and the community zoning committee. He was seldom home. Lonely, John's mother was heavily into volunteerism, and John says he spent more time with his housekeeper than with either parent.

John's past affected his marriage and effectively blocked any intimacy with his wife or his sons—Ron, twelve, and Timmy, nine. As a result of her lonely marriage, Melanie says that for about three years she thought of leaving John. "My husband shared his deepest feelings with me when we were dating, but after we were married, he seldom told me how he felt," says Melanie. "He didn't spend much time with the boys. He certainly didn't share his feelings. And he always said he'd play ball with them or take them fishing. But he never did."

Not only was John a workaholic like his father, but when he was home, he was often negative with his sons, particularly Timmy who had dyslexia. "I was especially worried about Timmy when his teacher called and said he'd been hitting the younger boys," says Melanie.

While Melanie was considering divorce, she clung to the hope that she and John could get help and could some day become emotionally close. Deeply religious, Melanie was not comfortable with divorce. She felt trapped in her marriage, true, but in her heart she had to admit that both she and John were responsible for the sterility of their union. One day, feeling desperate, she confided in several friends who met with her to pray.

As Melanie became more open with these friends, her anger at John surfaced and she confronted her husband.

"I was shocked at the intensity of my rage," says Melanie, "but I had bottled up my anger too long." Surprised at the depth of his wife's feelings, John spent even more time away from home.

During this time when Melanie was becoming more honest about her emotional pain, a series of crises occurred, increasing the marital pressure. John's father died, John lost a lot of money in the stock market, and Timmy, riding his bike home from soccer practice, was struck by a car. For several days he hovered between life and death.

John, who never cried, sobbed when he first saw his son's broken body in intensive care. As Timmy floated in and out of consciousness, Melanie, beside herself with fear and grief, watched her husband decompose before her. "He kept saying, 'Now I won't be able to take Timmy on that fishing trip I promised him.' It was all that I could do to keep myself from telling him that he seldom did any of the things he promised with either of the boys."

Following Timmy's accident, Melanie and John experienced love from different individuals from their church. Their pastor visited them at the hospital, and when he put his hand on John's shoulder to comfort him, John broke down and cried. "During those days following Timmy's accident, John's defenses started to crumble," says Melanie. "I guess it was the combination of his own father's death and the near loss of our son."

Melanie and John spent long hours together, driving to the hospital and caring for Timmy at home as he slowly recovered from the accident. John began to play basketball with Ron during early evenings and to linger with his wife over coffee, struggling to share his feelings—his anger, grief, and regret over his relationship with his father and his sorrow over his lack of involvement in his sons' lives. Melanie was able to reach past her anger and her unmet needs to reclaim some of the love she had felt earlier for her husband.

John also attended a retreat at their church and on this weekend had an intense religious experience. "I had not wanted to go," says John, "but as I listened to men talk about God as Father, I realized that I hated my father. At the same time, I yearned to be close to him. I also knew that I would have to forgive him. As I struggled to forgive him, I began to feel God loved me."

After that weekend, John and Melanie continued to work on their marriage. They sought professional help, and in time John made the connection between his father's rejection and his lack of any intimate involvement with his own sons. Also, he and Melanie learned to speak openly from their deepest selves. And Melanie, who once considered leaving her husband, now says, "John is changing. Now he wants to be close to me and the boys. He is meeting my emotional needs."

John told Melanie recently, "I can't believe we've been married fifteen years. Our marriage gets better all the time." And Melanie? She agrees.

World Enough and Time

A woman's whole life
is a history of the affections.

Washington Irving

Contrary to the prevailing cultural attitude, it is not inevitable that the mother at home fall hopelessly behind her careerist counterparts in the race for the good life.

I realize what I have just said contradicts the media portrayal of the mother at home. I remember a television program several years ago in which Sally Jessy Raphael forecast a bleak future for any mother who sacrifices career for family. Sally said if a woman stays home until age forty, no corporation will hire her. No one challenged Sally Jessy that day. One sensed she had touched a nerve since the audience and guests failed to respond. Many today fear that the mother at home will lose ground in the job market. This fear that they may be unemployable or have to take mediocre jobs in their forties keeps many women tied to the marketplace.

Molly's Dilemma

How does this fear affect the professional woman who is at home? I have before me a letter I received recently from a mother who is a physician in Colorado. She says that because she had her first child prior to the end of her internship, she has never practiced medicine full-time. Now she has four children, and the youngest is twenty months old. This mother has chosen to stay home and has even been homeschooling her older children. But while she admits her roles as "wife, mother, teacher, homemaker, bookkeeper for the medical practice" completely fill her time, she is not happy.

Molly is torn. While she doesn't have time to work even part-time (maybe later), she worries she is losing ground in her profession and may never catch up. "I feel a constant burden about this," Molly writes in a letter she composed at midnight, when the house was finally quiet.

Molly, like many other women, is caught on the horns of a dilemma. Home by choice because she believes her children need her, she is still anxious and afraid. What is she to do?

When I responded to Molly's letter, I told her I understood how she felt. I had those feelings myself when my children were in elementary school and junior high. Sometimes I asked Don, "What should I do?" He always suggested I continue doing what I felt was best for our family—pursue my at-home writing career and be available to the girls. "But," my husband ended each conversation, "Become wholehearted about your life or you will miss the *best* that this period of your life has to offer."

Career and Kids

An article in *Ms* by Edith Fierst says that many of today's successful women took years off to rear their children.

Fierst writes that Sandra Day O'Connor, Jeane Kirkpatrick, and Patricia Wald, chief judge of the U.S. Court of Appeals, spent between five and fifteen years out of the labor force. These women obviously didn't suffer in the work force because of years spent at home.

Some of the women Fierst interviewed even felt they returned to the work force too soon. Wald stayed home for ten years and only worked part-time when she went back to work. Yet when she was asked if she would do the same thing all over again, she said she would have stayed home longer, "for the benefit of the youngest child and not have pushed herself so hard."

The fifty women Fierst interviewed, who were in such careers as medicine, psychology, government, science, and teaching, did not regret they had devoted years to nurturing their young children. Said one, "As I get older, my children and family life become more important. Raising children is hard—and I'm glad I didn't miss it."

While most of the women in Fierst's study felt part-time employment was ideal for mothers (it kept their self-esteem high and enabled them to maintain contacts), even those mothers who stayed home full-time fared well returning to the work force. One, a lawyer who spent ten years at home full-time, became a vice-president of an Illinois firm. Another mother who stayed home for twenty-one years became an editor for an environmental protection publication. The women felt "their relatively advanced age was a help in finding a good job, because they had the advantage of experience with life, if not paid work."[1]

Perhaps it will comfort Molly and others like her to know many women pursue satisfying careers once they return to the work force. Granted, Molly may have to take a year or so to "catch up" professionally, but she will find she can draw on her earlier medical training, plus the experience she's acquired at home as a mother. Molly can, in fact, have several careers in her lifetime.

Life After Forty

We women have always had it better than men. While men struggle with career in their twenties and thirties, only to turn toward relationships in their forties and fifties, we women, because of our biological clock, establish our marital and family connections during our twenties and thirties. Then in our forties and fifties, when men are turning homeward, we can begin to focus on productive ventures outside our homes. Unlike the single-minded male who discovers the value of relationships in midlife, a woman can have multiple careers throughout her lifetime if she desires, and she will have had the boon of establishing nourishing, deep connections early on.

So Sally Jessy Raphael is wrong. Any woman who takes time off for her family is not washed up and ready to be sent to pasture at age forty. Many women who take years off reenter the work force successfully. Of course, not all women wish to go back to work once their kids leave home. Some enjoy the fruits of their labors and spend their time rediscovering husbands, taking vacations, picking up new interests. My friend Joanna, who raised five children, now enjoys spending time at her lakeside cottage, both with family and alone. Sitting on the dock, Joanna says, "I deserve this."

So what possibilities exist for post-menopausal women whose kids are raised and who feel that a productive segment of life lies before them—women at the late summer of life?

Dream a New Dream

This is time to dream a new dream. The tyranny of the biological clock is past. The dream of intimacy and family has been realized. If her marriage is in good shape and her children are reasonably whole, a woman brings to this stage of her life tremendous drive and energy. No longer having to balance the demands of her multiple roles, a woman "of a certain age" can simplify her life and pursue the things she's passionately interested in. She is, as one older woman said, ready to look beyond her home and "save the world."

In my own life, I focused my energies on further education. I had wanted to get my Ph.D. in my twenties but felt sidetracked once I had children. Then I couldn't ignore their incessant needs to work on a doctorate. When Holly was born, I was finishing my masters in English at the University of Buffalo. One day I went in to talk to one of my professors, and we were soon discussing my academic future. When he found out I had just had a baby, he leaned forward, planted his elbows on his desk, and said firmly, "What you should do now is push *hard*. Finish your Ph.D. while your child is young and then you can have a career in academia."

He had obviously never been a nursing mother! Even as I listened, I was calculating just how much time I had left before Holly's next feeding. Weeks later, when I sat for the comprehensive exam that separated the doctoral sheep from the masters goats, I was among the first to leave. How could I concentrate on *Huckleberry Finn* and the novel's place in American literature when my breasts ached and were starting to leak? Instead, I rushed home to breastfeed my screaming baby.

Enrolling at Georgetown at forty-two, I felt free at last to slip into fourth gear and, as my family says, "chew up the earth." I became single-minded in a way I had never been before. This was reflected in my performance: I became a far better student than I had been in my early twenties. When the day came that I defended my doctoral dissertation to the psychology faculty, I was anxious but exhilarated: I had finally achieved a long deferred dream.

Other women take different routes in dreaming a new dream.

I have been fortunate enough to get to know Phyllis Schlafly, founder and president of Eagle Forum, a national organization that takes credit for defeating the Equal Rights Amendment. Since Eagle Forum's inception some twenty years ago, Phyllis has marshaled other politically active women to lobby in their local and state governments for traditional values.

The organization is a powerful voice in conservative politics today on such issues as abortion, sex education in the schools, values clarification, child care, and parental leave. As president of Eagle Forum, Phyllis is often invited to the White House to attend meetings with the president, and she regularly confers with other movers and shakers in government.

According to her biographer, Carol Felsenthal, who wrote *The Sweetheart of the Silent Majorty*, Phyllis was valedictorian of her high school graduating class and the recipient of a Phi Beta Kappa key at college. She also worked full-time while putting herself through college and graduate school. After she graduated from Washington University in St. Louis, Phyllis attended Radcliffe where she obtained a masters degree in government.

Years later she brought this same formidable intellect and reservoir of energy to the task of mothering, teaching all of her six children to read before they entered school in second grade. The six Schlafly children reflect the accomplishments of both parents (Fred Schlafly graduated from Harvard Law School): two are lawyers, one is a physician, one holds a Ph.D. in mathematics, another a college degree in electrical engineering, and the youngest, Anne, has her own catering business.

Phyllis founded Eagle Forum in 1975 when she was fifty-one. And when she was criticized for testifying before the Senate without a law degree, Phyllis enrolled in law school at St. Louis University in her fifties. She graduated near the top of her class.

Whatever one feels about Phyllis Schlafly or her politics, this woman is a superlative example of someone who adheres to traditional values and fights for what she believes. She stayed home, raised her children, and then moved into a wider arena. She is now a national spokesperson, and her organization has some eighty thousand committed members.

Another woman who lived a modest, unassuming life until midlife and who has had a profound influence on the world is Mother Teresa of Calcutta. Mother Teresa cannot properly be called a mother at all—she never married or bore children—yet there is hardly a more nurturing figure alive today than this woman who, until she retired recently, ministered to the poor and dying. Mother Teresa was a school teacher until her late thirties. Then she received her second call: "The call within a call . . . to minister to the poorest of the poor."[3] Leaving the Foret convent of Calcutta, she took to the streets. According to Malcolm Muggeridge, Mother Teresa "stepped out with a few rupees in her pocket, made her way to the poorest, wretchedest quarter of the city, found a lodging there, gathered together a few abandoned children—there were plenty to chose from—and began her ministry of love."[4]

It is ironic that in an age when charity, nurture, and volunteerism are devalued and children are viewed as impediments to the fulfilled life, a woman receives the Nobel Peace Prize for nurturing the young and caring for the poor, the helpless, the dying. What many women have always done in their nuclear and extended families, Mother Teresa is doing for the family of humankind. And she has lived this enormously productive life in response to a second call that came when she was ready to dream a new dream.

It is not unusual for women writers to finally achieve success in midlife and beyond. Although Madeleine L'Engle had published four novels in her twenties and continued to write during her thirties, major success as a writer came to her only in her forties with the publication of her award-winning *A Wrinkle in Time*. Margaret Craven, a writer who has struggled with blindness, published her first novel *I Heard the Owl Call My Name* at the age of sixty-nine.

Another writer/mother began writing the novel that would rock a nation when she was forty-one. Bearing seven children in fourteen years, Harriet Beecher Stowe had little time for writing during the early years of her children's lives. And when she started her famous book, her family was not only broke but Stowe's inner resources were also depleted. Less than a year before she sat down to write *Uncle Tom's Cabin*, her young son Charlie had died. Stowe would later say about this experience, "It was at his dying bed and at his grave that I learned what a poor slave mother may feel when her child is taken away from her."[5] According to Russel Nye, the themes of mother love and separation run throughout Stowe's famous novel.[6]

This wife and mother wrote "swiftly and at white heat" in the early 1850s out of the recollections of her early life. In the process she created a "moral weapon" used in the war against slavery. Not only was Stowe's book the first American novel to sell more than a million copies, but Charles Summer credited Stowe with Lincoln's election as president,[7] and President Lincoln is purported to have remarked when he met Stowe, "So this is the little lady who wrote the book that started this great war."

Although Stowe made her major contribution to literature in her forties, another woman who achieved international fame did not even begin the career that would make her famous until she was in her late seventies.

Born in 1860, Anna Mary Robertson worked on her parents' farm and left home at twelve to become a "hired girl," cooking and cleaning for other families for the next fifteen years.[8] After Anna married in 1887, she had ten children, five of whom died. Eventually, she and her husband settled on a farm in New York state near Albany. Only after her husband died did Anna begin to "keep busy and to pass the time away" by painting.

Anna Mary Robertson, better known as Grandma Moses, was discovered by art collector Louis Caldor in 1938 when he saw her paintings hanging in a drugstore near Hoosier Falls, New York. Soon Grandma Moses was an international figure in the arts whose paintings were shown in New York, Washington, D.C., and Europe. She was interviewed by newscaster Edward R. Murrow and visited President Truman at the White House. Moreover, she made the cover of *Time* when she celebrated her one-hundredth birthday. This woman, called one of the greatest folk artists of all time, painted scenes she remembered from her youth: wash day, a hurricane at home, Christmas at home, Hoosier Falls in the winter.

Obviously unimpressed with herself, Grandma Moses said of her gift: "If I didn't start painting, I would have raised chickens."[9]

When she was a child her father told Anna Mary he dreamt he was in a large hall and people were clapping their hands and shouting. Then he saw Anna Mary walking on the shoulders of men. Grandma Moses thought of this dream years later when she became famous and received mail from around the world. She did, at the end of her life, "walk on the shoulders of men." She was loved and venerated by ordinary people, as well as by the rich and powerful.

Poet Archibald MacLeish wrote of Grandma Moses in 1948: "It is a great virtue in any artist to be what he is, whatever it is that has made him so, whether place or time or bad luck or good or a sound heart or no heart at all. Because Grandma Moses is what she is so sharply and so briskly and so simply . . . she is a true painter to be approached with honor and respect."[10]

To be truly oneself is to be an original. Only as we become ourselves are we in a position to give to others truly—to share our gifts, to shower little acts of love and mercy on those who need it, to speak with a voice that needs to be heard. But we must remember that Grandma Moses did not set out to be what she was—to find herself. Rather, she set out at age twelve *to live a life.* And she lived a life replete with family, husband, children, and homey experiences long before immortalizing them in her paintings.

We do not become ourselves overnight. We do it year by year, building act upon act, word upon word. But as we live our days honestly, listening to our hearts, walking by our principles, we can hope to be productive individuals until death.

A friend who's sixty-six said in a reflective moment, "I don't want to sit around as I grow older. I want to live a useful life until I die." This is the Judeo-Christian concept of aging—that we serve God and others and "die on our feet."

But what if we listen to the siren's call and sacrifice our family relationships for career or anything else, for that matter? Then we may move into old age with crippling regret.

One woman realized too late she had neglected her ties with her only child while she poured her considerable energies into her career. "I kept him up all night before he left for Tulane," Sally said, "telling him how sorry I was I had been absent for much of his life. Even when I was home, I was so preoccupied, so driven." Her son patiently listened to his mother's soliloquy of regret as he packed his bags that last night at home, but his life there in the house on Hamden Road was over. What comfort, really, could he give his mother at this late hour?

As women, we can't ignore our human connections, except at real peril. Nor can we ignore our intelligence and gifts except at great personal cost. Yet it is possible to give our families our valuable time and personal commit-ment. We can have it all—but not all at once. And if we live each day fully, we won't look back over the terrain of our lives with emotional pain because we were inaccessible to our families while our children were at home. Instead, we will feel blessed as we watch our children leave home, marry, and start their own families. We will feel part of a great cosmic scheme for families.

In the winter of her life, Grandma Moses wrote, "I look back on my life like a good day's work, it was done and I feel satisfied with it. I was happy and contented. . . and life is what we make it, always has been, always will be."[11]

—◆—⫶⟨⬦⟩⫶—◆—

The Legacy

His living has given so much more than
his dying could ever take away.
Jack Owen (speaking about his father)

Christmas 1990. Welcome to Lancaster, Pennsylvania. People bury their frozen chins deeper into their coats as they file into the Willow Street Fire Hall. Well over a hundred people have assembled for a Christmas dinner, and the surrounding streets are jammed with cars, many bearing out-of-state plates. Though they come from such far-flung places as Texas, Florida, and California, these people share a common bond: they are the descendants or in-laws of one couple, Harvey and Martha Owen.

"At first we were together every year because our parents wanted it that way," says eighty-five-year-old Mary Owen Clark. "Now we do it as a sort of tribute to them and because we enjoy it."[1]

What sort of couple inspires such familial pride and

loyalty? Harvey and Martha were an unusual duo. Martha was seventeen when she married her twenty-one-year-old former school teacher in West Jefferson, North Carolina in 1901. Settling in Lancaster, Harvey traded schoolteaching for small business ownership, first buying a dairy and later a grocery store. Harvey and Martha loved children and had twelve of their own. Though their family was large, the children remember happy childhoods and lots of individual attention.

"We all felt we were special," says Stella Owen Morrison. "When we grew up and talked about our parents, we were surprised to discover that *each* felt like the best-loved child." Maybe this was because Martha would dodge the question, "Who do you love the best?" by saying: "The one who's sick until he's well, the one who's gone until he's back among the rest."

Probably, however, the parents' love was best communicated by their actions. Harvey polished twelve pairs of shoes nightly and, as befits a former schoolteacher, tutored his and the neighbor children. Martha loved for her children to bring their friends home for dinner. "We never thought about the work or inconvenience this caused her," says Stella, "because at our house there was always room for one more." To keep her family close, Martha instigated the yearly Christmas dinner that was held in the family home until the 1940s. When the family outgrew the home, the Owens moved their celebration first to a school, then to a fire hall.

Though the family had little money, the children didn't realize it as they grew up. "Daddy would always find a nickel for you if you needed it," remembers Stella. What they did have, the Owens shared with others. Harvey and Martha welcomed five cousins who came to live with them to attend school in Lancaster. And when Martha got the first washing machine in the neighborhood, she invited her relatives to use it. Even in old age, Harvey and Martha made quilts together each year, one for each of their children and several for the local hospital.

In addition to possessing a generous spirit, Harvey and Martha were firm, but not harsh, disciplinarians. The parents' open hands could occasionally come down on their children's posteriors. When Stella, at age two, threw a bowl of oatmeal at her father, she was spanked. Worth was put under the dining room table when he hit a younger child. Most often, though, Harvey just talked to the offending child.

"He was not a pacifist, but he hated brutality," remembered son Jack. Says Mary, "Our parents disciplined us with feeling and care. They didn't fly into a rage and bawl you out." Once Stella broke the midnight curfew. The next day, as she was standing in the kitchen rolling biscuits, her father came in and said kindly, "You were out a little late; I don't think I'd stay out that late again." She didn't.

In addition to modeling gentleness and self-control, Harvey and Martha showed their children how to have a happy marriage. Both Mae and Stella remember their parents had a cooperative, loving union. Additionally, neither countermanded the other. "When mother made suggestions," says Mary, "Daddy didn't argue." "But she made good suggestions," counters Stella. Once Harvey was about to prune raspberry bushes with his son-in-law Frank, and Martha asked him to wait to allow the children to pick the remaining berries. "Without missing a beat," says Mary, "Daddy turned to Frank and said, 'Let's go trim the grape vines instead.' "

While they had a harmonious marriage, Harvey and Martha were not perfect. In fact, there was one thing they never agreed on. Martha was a Baptist while Harvey was Methodist. Although they worshiped in different churches, this was never a point of contention. At home they presented a united front: Harvey read the Bible aloud each evening and the family sang hymns together.

To ensure that each child did not get lost in the pack, the family had a pattern that fostered strong attachments. Whenever a new baby was born, Mae, the oldest, took the dethroned sibling into her own bed and cuddled him. And when a child was sick, not only did Martha care for the child but Harvey brought his son or daughter favors from the store he owned.

Both Harvey and Martha come from strong, highly functional families. Stella remembers that though her grandmother died when her mother was four, an aunt quickly moved in to nurture the motherless children. Later, Martha's father remarried, and the stepmother got on so well with the stepchildren that Stella says she was a teenager before she knew her grandmother was actually her stepgrandmother. Martha and her stepmother were close, and Martha remained close to her aunt, the surrogate mother, as well. And Harvey came from a close, intact family. In fact, he and Martha chose to live with Harvey's parents when they were first married. Recalls Mary, "It was like a picnic to be with them."

Psychologists Belsky and Pensky note that happy marriages beget happy marriages.[2] This has been part of the rich legacy Harvey and Martha have passed on to their children. Among their twelve children only one divorced. In an era of easy divorce, five couples have stayed together for more than fifty years. Mary says she and her husband

Frank, who have just celebrated their sixty-fifth anniversary, are trying to emulate her parents, whose marriage lasted nearly three-quarters of a century.

In addition to creating their own strong families, Harvey and Martha's children have contributed much to American society. Sixteen members of this family have served their country in the armed forces. Additionally, the Owen children and their descendants have been pastors, teachers, nurses, missionaries, secretaries, salesmen, beauticians, carpenters, chefs, bank executives, research personnel, artists, and horse trainers, among others.

Today the 189 descendants are scattered throughout twenty-one states, the District of Columbia, Australia, and Ecuador.

Even the third generation has benefited from the lives of this unique couple. Mary's daughter, Sidney Clark, captured something of the richness of her family's legacy when she wrote "On the Death of My Grandfather" when Harvey died.

> White-haired patriarch
> He tended grape arbors
> and knew his books,
> told summer secrets
> and laughed with her.
> Long winter nights
> he built dream houses
> with windows going everywhere
> and we could reach and climb
> to find the limits of our minds
> in the closeness of a time.
> He knitted wool-like love
> and spread the blanket

over all he knew
or hung it from a cloud
to block a sometime shadow
on the sun.

Now friends throw flowers
to the sky
and we
sharing each other
hold fast his legacy.

The legacy. As parents we invariably give our children a legacy of memories. *A sense of home or a deep, abiding feeling of homelessness.* It is only as we consider our children's well-being a high priority—and are willing to make the essential sacrifices—that we will give them a rich legacy of memories to treasure throughout their lives. In the process, we will not only strengthen society, but we will affect future generations as well.

As the French Noble Laureate Francois Mauriac has said, "We are moulded and remoulded by those who have loved us; and though the love may pass, we are nevertheless their work, for good or ill."

Notes

Introduction: The Inner Home

1. Allen H. Platt, "The Importance of Home," *Time*, 28 January 1991, 9.

2. Anthony Storr, *Churchill's Black Dog, Kafka's Mice and Other Phenomenon of the Mind* (New York: Ballantine Books, 1988), 18-19.

3. Anthony Storr, *Solitude* (New York: Ballantine Books, 1988), 112.

4. Vivien Noakes, *Edward Lear* (London: Fontana, 1985), 14.

5. Ibid., 107.

6. Storr, *Solitude*, 113.

7. Joyce Maynard, "Home Stretch," *Elle*, October 1990, 202-206.

Chapter 1: Homeward Bound

1. J. Bowlby, *Attachment*, vol. 1 of *Attachment and Loss*, 2d ed. (New York: Basic Books, 1982), 177.

2. Ibid., xiii.

3. Sigmund Freud, *Outline of Psychoanalysis*, SE 23 (London: Hogarth Press, 1940), 188.

4. B. Egeland and E. A. Farber, "Infant-Mother Attachment: Factors Related to Development and Change Over Time," *Child Development*, 55 (1984):753-771.

5. Alan Stroufe and Everett Waters, "Attachment as an Organizational Construct," *Child Development*, 48 (1977): 1186.

6. Ibid.

7. John Bowlby, *Separation: Anxiety and Anger*, vol. 2 of *Attachment and Loss* (New York: Basic Books, 1973), 204.

8. Armand Nicholi, "The Fractured Family: Following It into the Future," *Christianity Today*, 25 May 1979, 11.

9. Ibid.

10. Selma Fraiberg, "Ghosts in the Nursery," in *Selected Writings of Selma Fraiberg*, ed. Louis Fraiberg (Columbus, Ohio: Ohio State University Press, 1987), 102.

11. Ibid., 135.

12. B. J. Cohler and H. V. Grunebaum, *Mothers, Grandmothers and Daughters* (New York: Wiley, 1981).

Chapter 2 : Forging Attachments

1. Evelyn. B. Thoman and Sue Browder, *Born Dancing* (New York: Harper and Row, 1987), 5.

2. Ibid.

3. Ibid., 127-129.

4. John Bowlby, *Attachment*, vol. 1 of *Attachment and Loss* (New York: Basic Books, 1969), 199-202.

5. John Bowlby, address given to the American Psychiatric Association (APA) in Washington, D.C., 1986.

6. Michael E. Lamb, "The Development of Mother-Infant and Father-Infant Attachment in the Second Year of Life," *Developmental Psychology*, 13 (1977): 637-648.

7. John Bowlby, *A Secure Base* (New York: Basic Books, 1988), 11.

8. Ibid.

9. Michael Lamb, "The Development of Parent-Infant Attachments in the First Two Years of Life." In ed. F. A. Pederson *The Father-Infant Relationship* (New York: Praeger, 1980), 35.

10. Ibid.

11. Ibid., 11.

12. Ibid.

13. John Bowlby, *Separation: Anxiety and Anger*, vol. 2 of *Attachment and Loss* (New York: Basic Books, 1973), 204.

14. Ibid, 204-205.

15. John Bowlby, *Loss: Sadness and Depression*, vol. 3 of *Attachment and Loss* (New York: Basic Books, 1980), 55.

16. Ibid., 231.

17. Bowlby, *Separation*, 208.

18. Bowlby, *Secure Base*, 28.

19. Bowlby, address given at APA convention, 1986.

20. Bowlby, *Secure Base*, 11.

21. Fritz Goossens and M. H. von Ijzendoorn, "Quality of Infants' Attachments to Professional Caregivers: Relation to Infant-Parent Attachment and Day Care Characteristics," *Child Development*, 61 (1990): 832-837.

22. Graeme Russell, "Shared Caregiving Families: An Australian Study," in *Nontraditional Families: Parenting and Child Development*, ed. M. E. Lamb (Hillsdale, N. J.: Lawrence Erlbaum Associates, 1982), 139-164.

23. Graeme Russell, "Primary Care Giving and the Role Sharing Fathers," ed. M. E. Lamb, *The Father's Role* (New York: Wiley & Sons, 1986), 31.

Chapter 3: Mother Care or Other Care?

1. Sandra Scarr, *Mother Care/Other Care* (New York: Warner Books, 1984), 77.

2. Ibid., 231-232.

3. Ibid., 232.

4. Jay Belsky, "Infant Day Care: A Cause for Concern," *Zero to Three*, September 1986, 3.

5. Jay Belsky, "Risks Remain," *Zero to Three*, Special Reprint, 22.

6. John Bowlby, address given to the American Psychiatric Association convention, Washington, D.C., 1986.

7. Robert Karen, "Becoming Attached," *The Atlantic Monthly*, February 1990, 47.

8. M. D. S. Ainsworth et al., *Patterns of Attachment* (Hillsdale, N. J.: Lawrence Erlbaum Associates, 1978), viii.

9. Ibid., 55-63.

10. Mary Ainsworth, "Patterns of Infant-Mother Attachments: Antecedents and Effects of Development," *Bulletin of New York Academy of Medicine*, 61 (November 1985): 776.

11. Karen, "Becoming Attached," 50.

12. Ainsworth et al., *Patterns of Attachment*, 59.

13. Ainsworth, "Infant-Mother Attachments," 777.

14. Karen, "Becoming Attached," 50.

15. Mary Main, "Avoidance of the Attachment Figure in

Infancy: Descriptions and Interpretations," *Behavioral Development: The Bielegeld Interdisciplinary Project* (New York: Cambridge University Press, 1981), 31-59.

16. Erik Larson, "When You Have to Say Goodbye," *Parents*, March 1990, 104.

17. William Damon, *Social and Personality Development* (New York: W. W. Norton & Co., 1983), 35.

18. Ibid., 34.

19. Erik Larson, "WhenYou Have to Say Goodbye," 104.

20. Judith Viorst, *Necessary Losses* (New York: Simon and Schuster, 1986), 31.

21. Pamela Schwartz, "Length of Day Care Attendance and Attachment Behavior in Eighteen-month-old Infants," *Child Development*, 54 (1983): 1073-1078.

22. D. Wille and J. Jacobsen, "The Influence of Maternal Employment, Attachment Patterns, Extra-familial Child Care and Previous Experiences with Peers or Early Peer Interaction" (Paper presented at the International Conference in Infant Studies, New York, 1984.)

23. P. Barglow, B. E. Vaughn, and N. Molitor, "Effects of Maternal Absence Due to Employment on the Quality of Infant-Mother Attachment in a Low-risk Sample," *Child Development*, 58 (1987): 945-954.

24. P. L. Chase-Lansdale and M. T. Owen, "Maternal Employment in a Family Context: Effects on Infant-Mother and Infant-Father Attachments, *Child Development*, 58 (1987): 1505-1512.

25. J. Belsky and M. Rovine, "Nonmaternal Care in the First Year of Life and the Security of the Infant-Parent Attachment, *Child Development*, 59 (1987): 157-167.

26. J. C. Schwarz, R. G. Strickland, and G. Krolick, "Infant Day Care: Behavioral Effects at Preschool Age," *Developmental Psychology*, 10 (1974): 502-506.

27. Ron Haskins, "Public School Aggression among Children with Varying Day Care Experience," *Child Development*, 56 (1985): 700.

28. Carolee Howes, "Can the Age of Entry into Child Care and the Quality of Child Care Predict Adjustment in

Kindergarten?" *Developmental Psychology,* 26 (1990): 292-303.

29. Jay Belsky, Infant Attachment Research Seminar, Washington, D.C., 4-5 February 1991.

30. P. Forman, "Day Care Diseases," *Family Policy,* a publication of the Family Research Council, Washington, D.C., May/June 1989, 1-4.

31. Wendy Dreskin, "Day Care: A Child's View" in *Who Will Rock the Cradle,* ed. Phyllis Schlafly (Washington, D.C.: Eagle Forum Education and Defense Fund, 1989), 127.

32. Ibid., 130.

33. Selma Fraiberg, *Every Child's Birthright: In Defense of Mothering* (New York: Bantam Books, 1977), 34.

34. Ibid., 98.

35. Ibid., 102.

Chapter 4: Fall from Grace

1. M. E. Lamb, "Maternal Employment and Child Development: A Review," in *Non-Traditional Families: Parenting and Child Development,* ed. M. E. Lamb (Hillsdale, N. J.: Lawrence Erlbaum Associates, 1982), 46.

2. Ibid., 48.

3. Douglas Besharov and Michelle Dally, *Public Opinion,* November-December 1986, 48-51.

4. Barbara Ehrenreich, "Sorry, Sisters, This Is Not the Revolution," *Time,* Fall 1990, 15.

5. Sylvia Porter, "Housewives Contribute Billions to Economy," *Los Angeles Times* Syndicate.

6. Lisa Leff, "Stay at Home Mothers Say They Feel Isolated," *Washington Post,* 7 December 1986.

7. Bob Greene, "The Woman in the Photograph," *Esquire,* June 1984, 23-24.

8. Ibid.

9. Claudia Wallis, "Women in the '90s," *Time,* 4 December 1989.

Chapter 5: Why Do Women Reject Motherhood?

1. Rhona Rapoport and Robert Rapoport, *Dual Career Families* (Baltimore: Penguin, 1971), 282.

2. Laurel Oliver, "The Relationships of Parental Attitudes and Parent Identification to Career and Homemaking Orientation in College Women," *Journal of Vocational Behavior,* 1 (1975): 1-12.

3. Margaret Hennig and Anne Jardin, *The Managerial Woman* (New York: Simon and Schuster, 1976), 130-132.

4. Ibid., 125.

5. Ibid., 123.

6. Ibid., 129.

7. M. J. Gerson, "The Lure of Motherhood," *Psychology of Women Quarterly,* 5 (2): 207-218.

8. Ibid., 217.

9. B. E. Lott, "Who Wants the Children? Some Relationships among Attitudes toward Children, Parents and the Liberation of Women," *American Psychologist,* 28 (1973): 573-582.

10. Marcia Cohen, *The Sisterhood* (New York: Fawcett-Columbine, 1988), 61.

11. Ibid., 58.

12. Ibid., 59.

13. Ibid., 69.

14. Ibid., 29.

15. Ibid., 31.

16. Ibid.

17. Ibid., 37.

18. Ibid., 38.

19. Germaine Greer, *Daddy, We Hardly Knew You* (New York: Knopf, 1990), 23.

20. Ibid., 38.

21. Cohen, *The Sisterhood,* 45.

22. Ibid., 50.

23. John Bowlby, *Making and Breaking of Affectional Bonds* (London: Tavistock, 1979), 139.

24. Cohen, *The Sisterhood,* 50.

25. Deborah Fallows, *A Mother's Work* (Boston: Houghton Mifflin, 1985), 206.

26. Greer, *Daddy, We Hardly Knew You,* 311.

Chapter 6: Do Older Kids Need Mother at Home?

1. Roper Center Review of Pubic Opinion, a 1989 poll of three thousand women. Reported in *USA Today*, 5 June 1990.

2. Anastasia Toufeis, "Struggling for Sanity," *Time*, 8 October 1990, 48.

3. Ann Landers, *Washington Post*, 18 November 1990.

4. Toufeis, "Struggling for Sanity," 48.

5. Richard Louv, *Childhood's Future* (Boston: Houghton Mifflin, 1990), 18.

6. Ibid., 17.

7. Ibid., 19.

8. Catherine O'Neill, "School's Out, Mom's Out, So's Dad," *Washington Post*, 21 October 1986, 13.

9. Armand Nicholi, "The Nontherapeutic Use of Psychoactive Drugs," *The New England Journal of Medicine*, 308 (April 1983): 925-933.

10. Ibid., 931f.

11. Ibid.

12. Jean L. Richardson et al, "Substance Use among Eighth Grade Students Who Take Care of Themselves after School," *Pediatrics*, 84 (1989): 556-565.

13. Ann C. Crouter, S. M. MacDermid, S. M. McHale, and M. Perry-Jenkins, "Parental Monitoring and Perceptions of Children's School Performance and Conduct in Dual and Single Earner Families," *Developmental Psychology*, 26 (1990): 649-657.

14. Michael Ryan, "Now They're at Harvard," *Parade*, 17 July 1988, 20.

15. Ibid.

16. Kevin B. MacDonald, *Social and Personality Adjustment* (New York: Plenum Press, 1988), 166.

17. Ibid., 163.

18. N. Kiell, *The Universal Experience of Adolescence* (New York: International Universities Press, 1964), 12.

19. Erik Erikson, *Childhood and Society* (New York: W. W. Norton, 1964), 262.

20. E. James Anthony, lecture given at the Department of Psychiatry, Georgetown University Hospital, Fall 1987.

21. M. F. Ehrenberg, D. N. Cox, and R. F. Koopman, "The

Prevalence of Depression in High School Students," *Adolescence,* 25 (Winter 1990): 905-912.

22. R. L. Simon and P. I. Murphy, "Sex Differences in the Causes of Adolescent Suicide and Ideation," *Journal of Adolescence,* 14 (1985): 423-434.

23. Larry Brain, lecture given at the Department of Psychiatry, Georgetown University Hospital, Fall 1987.

24. J. M. Mishne, *Clinical Work with Adolescents* (New York: The Free Press, 1986), 207.

25. Ibid., 208-209.

26. Ibid., 210

Chapter 7: CEOs in the Suburbs

1. Paul and Sarah Edwards, *Working from Home* (Los Angeles: Jeremy P. Tarches, Inc., 1990), 1.

2. Ibid.

3. Ibid., 2.

4. Alvin Toffler, *The Third Wave* (New York: William Morrow, 1980).

5. Ibid., 192.

6. "1982 Characteristics of Business Owners," U.S. Census Bureau, August 1987.

7. Marion Behr and Wendy Lazar, *Women Working at Home* (New Jersey: W. W. H. Press, 1981), 11.

8. Cherie Fuller, "Ways for Moms to Make Money at Home," *Focus on the Family Magazine,* January 1991, 2.

9. Edwards, *Working from Home,* 41.

10. "Selling Romance, British Style," *Time,* 21 December 1981, 66.

11. Edwards, *Working from Home,* 27.

12. Ibid., 38.

13. Fuller, "Make Money at Home," 3.

14. Edwards, *Working from Home,* 198.

Chapter 8: Home for a Season

1. Ruth Josselson, *Finding Herself* (San Francisco: Jossey-Bass, 1987), 26.

2. Carol Gilligan, *In a Different Voice* (Cambridge, Mass.:

Harvard University Press, 1982), 12.

3. Josselson, *Finding Herself,* 3.

4. Ibid., 170.

5. Ibid., 173.

6. Ibid.

7. Ibid., 185.

8. Carol Gilligan, *In a Different Voice,* 159.

9. Henry Gleitman, *Basic Psychology* (New York: W.W. Norton, 1987), 183.

Chapter 9: Women and Depression

1. Myrna M. Weissman, "Depression," in *Women and Psychotherapy,* ed. A. M. Brodsky and R. T. Hare-Mustin (New York: Guilford Press, 1980), 980.

2. Ibid., 98-99.

3. Ibid., 101-102.

4. P. D. McLean, "Behavioral Treatment of Depression," in *Behavior Modification,* ed. W. E. Craighead, A. E. Kazdin, and M. J. Mahoney (Boston: Houghton Mifflin, 1981), 223-241.

5. Maggie Scarf, *Unfinished Business: Pressure Points in the Lives of Women* (Garden City, N.Y.: Doubleday, 1980), 566-567.

6. Ibid., 4-5.

7. G. W. Brown and T. Harris, *Social Origins of Depression* (New York: The Free Press, 1978), 179.

8. Jay Belsky and Emily Pensky, "Developmental History, Personality and Family Relationships: Toward an Emergent Family System," in *Relationships within Families: Mutual Influences,* ed. R. Hinde and J. Stevenson-Hinde (Oxford, England: Oxford University Press, 1988), 203.

9. M. Lefkotiz and E. P. Tesiny, "Rejection and Depression: Prospective and Contemporaneous Analyses," *Developmental Psychology,* 20 (1984): 776-785.

10. Robert Leahy, "The Costs of Development: Clinical Implications," *The Development of the Self* (New York: Academic Press, 1985), 267-294.

11. David Burns, *Feeling Good: The New Mood Therapy* (New York: Morrow, 1980), 12.

12. Ibid.

13. Anne Stevenson, *Bitter Fame: A Life of Sylvia Plath* (New York: Viking, 1989), 265.

14. John Bowlby, lecture given at American Psychiatric Association Convention, Washington, D.C. May, 1986.

Chapter 10: Healing the Wounded Self

1. Nancy Friday, *My Mother/Myself* (New York: Dell Publishing, 1977), x.

2. Margaret Ricks, "The Social Transformation of Parental Behavior: Attachment across Generations," in *Growing Points of Attachment Theory and Research,* monographs of the Society for Research in Child Development, ed. Inge Bretherton and Everett Waters, vol. 50, nos. 1-2, 1985, 221.

3. Ibid., 220-221.

4. Ibid., 220.

5. Anthony Storr, *The Art of Psychotherapy* (New York: Routledge), 25.

6. Ibid., 73.

7. Ibid.

8. *Selected Writings of Selma Fraiberg,* ed. Louis Fraiberg (Columbus, Ohio: The State University Press, 1987), viii-ix.

9. Ibid., 139.

10. Ibid., 143.

11. Ibid., 149-150.

12. Ibid., 161.

13. Ibid., 162.

14. John Bowlby, talk given to physicians at the American Psychiatric Association convention, Washington, D.C., May 1986.

15. Karlen Lyons-Ruth et al., "Infants at Social Risk: Maternal Depression and Family Support Services as Mediators of Infant Development and Security of Attachment," *Child Development,* 61 (1990): 85-98.

16. Storr, *Art of Psychotherapy,* 157.

17. Roger Helle, "Getting to Be Somebody," *Guideposts,* April 1987, 3.

18. Ibid., 4.

19. Ibid., 5.

20. Jay Belsky and Emily Pensky, "Developmental History,

Personality and Family Relationships: Toward Our Emergent Family System," in *Relationships Within Families: Mutual Influences*, R. Hinde and J. Stevenson-Hinde (Oxford, England: Oxford University Press, 1988), 209.

Chapter 11: The Man in Her Life

1. Judith Viorst, *Necessary Losses* (New York: Simon and Schuster, 1986), 192.

2. Ibid.

3. Ibid.

4. Sam Allis, "What Do Men Really Want?" *Time*, Fall 1990, 80.

5. D. L. Shepherd-Look, "Sex Differentiation and the Development of Sex Roles," in *Handbook of Child Development*, ed. B. B. Wolman (Englewood Cliffs, N.J.: Prentice-Hall, 1982), 408.

6. Ibid., 408.

7. Michael Lamb, "Maternal Employment and Child Development: A Review," in *Non-Traditional Families: Parenting and Child Development*, ed. M. E. Lamb (Hillsdale, N.J.: Lawrence Erlbaum Associates, 1982), 57-58.

8. Carol Gilligan, *In a Different Voice* (Cambridge, Mass.: Harvard University Press, 1982), 173.

9. Michel Marriot, "Father Hunger," *Essence*, November 1990, 74.

10. Ibid.

11. Ibid., 116.

12. Bill Glass, speech given to Prison Fellowship staff in Reston, Va., Fall 1990.

Chapter 12: World Enough and Time

1. Edith Fierst, "Careers and Kids," *Ms*, May 1988, 62-64.

2. Carol Felsenthal, *The Sweetheart of the Silent Majority* (Chicago: Regnery Gateway, 1981), 33.

3. Malcolm Muggeridge, *Something Beautiful for God* (Garden City, N.Y.: Image Books, 1977), 5.

4. Ibid., 17.

5. Harriet Beecher Stowe, *Uncle Tom's Cabin* (New York: Simon and Schuster, 1963), ix.

6. Ibid., xiii.

7. Ibid.

8. "Biographical Sketch," in *Grandma Moses* (Washington, D.C.: National Gallery of Art, 1979), 14.

9. Ibid., 15.

10. Ibid., 9.

11. Ibid., 15.

Postscript: The Legacy

1. "Owen Clan Gathers, Celebrates in a Big Way," *Sunday News*, Lancaster, Pa., 16 December 1990, E-3.

2. Jay Belsky and Emily Pensky, "Developmental History, Personality and Family Relationships: Toward an Emergent Family System," in *Relationships within Families: Mutual Influences*, ed. R. Hinde and J. Stevenson-Hinde (Oxford, England: Oxford University Press, 1988), 198.

Index